Engaging Pupil Voice to Ensure that Every Child Matters
A Practical Guide

Pupil voice is at the heart of Every Child Matters and is the driving force in acknowledging the rights, voice and choice of children and young people today. This very practical up-to-the-minute book is an invaluable and essential resource for all those working directly with pupils in schools and other educational settings, who wish to strengthen the engagement of pupil voice in their every day practice. This book covers:

- the origin, concept and principles of pupil voice;
- the rights of children and young people in society today;
- how the latest pupil voice national surveys and reports inform ECM practice at whole school, classroom and community levels;
- effective practical approaches for gathering pupils' views and enhancing their participation to inform and influence ECM decision-making;
- evaluating the impact and outcomes of pupil voice on effecting change, in line with OFSTED and other national standards requirements.

Featuring helpful checklists, models of good practice, templates and photocopiable resources that can be used in pupil voice developmental work, this accessible and user-friendly guide is packed with useful information and advice, as well as offering suggestions for further reading, websites and resources.

Those who will find this book useful are leaders and managers of Every Child Matters, trainee and experienced teachers, teaching assistants, learning mentors, leading teachers and co-ordinators for Personalised Learning, PSHE and Citizenship, local authority Children's Services professionals working directly with schools and lecturers in higher education.

If every child and young person's view really matters, then every educational setting will value using this book.

Rita Cheminais is an independent consultant for Every Child Matters. She has written a number of valuable books in the area. These include *Every Child Matters: A New Role for SENCOs, Every Child Matters: A Practical Guide for Teachers* and *Every Child Matters: A Practical Guide for Teaching Assistants*. She is contactable on admin@ecm-solutions.org.uk and www.ecm-solutions.org.uk.

D1472838

Engaging Pupil Voice to Ensure that Every Child Matters

A Practical Guide

RITA CHEMINAIS

Routledge
Taylor & Francis Group

LONDON AND NEW YORK

First published 2008
by Routledge
2 Park Square, Milton Park, Abingdon, Oxon OX14 4RN

Simultaneously published in the USA and Canada
by Routledge
270 Madison Ave, New York, NY 10016

Routledge is an imprint of the Taylor & Francis Group, an informa business

British Library Cataloguing in Publication Data
A catalogue record for this book is available from the British Library

Library of Congress Cataloging in Publication Data
Cheminais, Rita.
  Engaging pupil voice to ensure that every child matters : a practical guide / Rita Cheminais.
    p. cm.
  ISBN 978–0–415–46854–1
  1. School improvement programs—Great Britain.   2. School management and organization—Great Britain.   3. Education—Standards—Great Britain.   I. Title.
  LB2822.84.G7C44 2008
  371.2′070942—dc22
  2008004922

ISBN10: 0-415-46854-X (pbk)
ISBN13: 978-0-415-46854-1 (pbk)

Typeset in Adobe Garamond by
RefineCatch Limited, Bungay, Suffolk
Printed and bound in Great Britain by
Bell & Bain Ltd, Glasgow

8/17/11

Dedication

This book is dedicated to my mother, Joan Cheminais, who though she was in hospital for the majority of the time during the writing of this book, has remained interested in the progress of my writing, and been keen to hear of my success in making a real difference to the lives of staff and pupils in schools.

Thank you for always being there for me, and I truly hope this will not be the last book of mine you will ever see published.

Contents

List of Figures and Tables

Figures

Tables

Acknowledgements

Thanks are due to the colleagues around the country whom I have had the pleasure to meet and work with on my travels to a number of local authorities, and who have inspired and encouraged me to continue to produce practical resources to support the implementation of the Every Child Matters initiative.

Of all the books I have written on Every Child Matters, this one on pupil voice is the most important.

Special thanks go to:

the outstanding and exceptional professionals in Tameside Services for Children and Young People who continue to support me in my writing;

the dedicated, dynamic and innovative headteachers in Tameside schools who have helped me to identify the practical resources necessary to strengthen pupil voice;

Philip Eastwood, AST for Initial Teacher Training at St Mary's and St Paul's CE Primary School in Knowsley who continues to plant the seed of an idea for my next book in the Every Child Matters series;

all the professionals from higher education institutions and educational publishing who have promoted and referred to my work;

Dr Monika Lee, Commissioning Editor, Georgina Korinek, Production Editor at Routledge/ David Fulton Education, and Gail Welsh, copy editor, for all their advice and support in making this book a reality.

Abbreviations

ASDAN	Award Scheme Development and Accreditation Network
AST	Advanced Skills Teacher
BT	British Telecommunications
CfBT	Centre for British Teachers
CPD	continuing professional development
CRAE	Children's Rights Alliance for England
CRC	Children's Research Centre
CRD	Children's Rights Director
CSCi	Commission for Social Care Inspection
CYPP	Children and Young People's Plan
CYPU	Children and Young People's Unit
DCSF	Department for Children, Schools and Families
DfEE	Department for Education and Employment
DfES	Department for Education and Skills
DH	Department of Health
DMYP	Deputy Member of Youth Parliament
DVD	digital versatile disc
ECHR	European Convention on Human Rights
ECM	Every Child Matters
ESRC	Economic and Social Research Council
ESSA	English Secondary Students Association
FE	Further Education
IIP	Investors in Pupils
INSET	in service training
IPPR	Institute of Public Policy Research
ITT	Initial Teacher Training
JRF	Joseph Rowntree Foundation
LA	local authority
LDD	learning difficulties and disabilities
LSC	Learning and Skills Council
MORI	Market & Opinion Research International
MYP	Member of Youth Parliament
NASEN	National Association for Special Educational Needs
NCB	National Children's Bureau
NCSL	National College for School Leadership
NFER	National Foundation for Educational Research
NHSS	National Healthy School Standard
NSF	National Service Framework

NSPCC	National Society for the Prevention of Cruelty to Children
NYA	National Youth Agency
OCRD	Office of the Children's Rights Director
OFSTED	Office for Standards in Education, Children's Services and Skills
PECS	picture exchange communication system
PIRLS	Progress in International Reading Literacy Study
PRU	Pupil Referral Unit
PSA	Parent Staff Association
PSHE	Personal, Social and Health Education
PTA	Parent Teacher Association
QCA	Qualifications and Curriculum Authority
RRS	Rights Respecting Schools
SCUK	School Councils United Kingdom
SEAL	social, emotional aspects of learning
SEF	self-evaluation form
SEN	special educational needs
SIP	School Improvement Partner
TDA	Training and Development Agency for Schools
TEC	Training and Enterprise Council
TES	*Times Educational Supplement*
TLRP	Teaching and Learning Research Programme
TV	television
UK	United Kingdom
UKYP	United Kingdom Youth Parliament
UN	United Nations
UNCRC	United Nations Convention on the Rights of the Child
UNICEF	United Nations International Children's Emergency Fund
USA	United States of America

The Aim of this Book

The aim of this book is to enable all those working directly with children and young people in schools and other educational settings such as Pupil Referral Units (PRUs), Further Education Colleges and Sixth Form Colleges to:

- understand the concept and principles of pupil voice;
- know the rights of children and young people;
- apply and transfer the main findings and recommendations from key national surveys and reports on pupil voice to inform whole school and classroom practice;
- identify appropriate strategies and approaches to engage and enhance pupil voice and participation in relation to Every Child Matters (ECM);
- develop and build upon existing good practice in pupil voice to ensure positive contributions are made by children and young people;
- know how to evaluate the impact of pupil voice in improving the ECM outcomes for children and young people.

Who the book is for?

- all trainee and qualified teachers, teaching assistants and learning mentors;
- leading teachers for Intervention, Gifted and Talented Education, Behaviour and Attendance;
- coordinators for PSHE, Citizenship, Inclusion, Personalised Learning and Extended Schools;
- senior leaders and managers with strategic responsibility for Every Child Matters;
- children's workforce frontline practitioners from education, health and social care working directly with pupils in schools and other educational settings;
- local authority school improvement officers and consultants responsible for leading Every Child Matters, Inclusion, PSHE, Citizenship, and the Healthy School Standard initiative;
- School Improvement Partners and Inspectors;
- senior lecturers in Higher Education responsible for the professional development of teachers, and others in the children's workforce.

How the format is designed to be used

The book provides a resource that can be used:

- to act as a quick point of reference for busy practitioners and senior leaders and managers in a range of educational settings and children's services;
- to inform pupil-led inclusive pupil voice policy and practice in a variety of educational settings;
- to enable pages to be photocopied for developmental purposes, within the purchasing institution or service.

Introduction

There has been a growing commitment to, and a renewal in the popularity of pupil voice at a national and local level, since the publication of the government's Green Paper *Every Child Matters* in 2003, and with the implementation of the Children Act 2004, and the introduction of the National Service Framework for children, young people and maternity services core standards in 2004.

Pupil voice is the 'buzz word' of the twenty-first century, as well as being an essential aspect of personalisation and inclusion. The citizenship curriculum, the revised OFSTED inspection framework, and the National Healthy School Standard (NHSS) supporting Personal, Social and Health Education (PSHE) have all helped to emphasise the importance of pupil voice and participation. Pupil voice is central to the *Every Child Matters* (ECM) agenda, which honours and recognises the rights of children and young people enacted through the five ECM outcomes: be healthy; stay safe; enjoy and achieve; make a positive contribution; and achieve economic well-being. Every Child Matters places a moral obligation on schools and other educational settings to acknowledge the rights, voice and choice of its pupils.

Members of any school's children's workforce from teachers, teaching assistants, learning mentors and lunchtime supervisors to frontline staff working directly with pupils from education, health and social care services, need to see pupil voice as being integral to the success of their work in improving outcomes for children and young people. The police, social workers, medical practitioners and counsellors already have the skills and expertise in securing and listening to the views of children and young people. They have useful practice to exchange with teachers in schools, whose training traditionally has not adequately prepared them to work more collaboratively and democratically with pupils as partners in the learning process. One 14-year-old girl commented in the Children's Society Good Childhood Inquiry into attitudes towards learning:

> If they (*teachers*) maybe took a minute to think about the comments we make, they would make school life for a lot of children much happier and more enjoyable.
>
> (2007c: 5)

Clearly, the message here is that teachers need to be prepared to listen to, and learn from, the pupils with whom they work.

Schools and children's services need to acknowledge that children and young people do have a right to be consulted and taken seriously when decisions about them are being made.

The Young People's Advisory Group, which contributed to the government's guidance on *Working Together: Giving Children and Young People a Say*, commented:

> We have a right to be heard too.
>
> The only way we can change things is to make sure that people who make decisions know

what we think and what we want. If we don't get involved we are likely to get only what other people want.

(2004b)

Ed Balls, the Secretary of State for Children, Schools and Families, considers it is good to hear the views and aspirations of children and young people, and to keep listening to them, in order to ensure they remain a priority locally and nationally. The voice and views of children and young people informed the government's Children's Plan which was published in December 2007 (DCSF 2007c). This plan reflects the general principles and Articles of the United Nations Convention on the Rights of the Child (UNCRC), and is aligned to the five Every Child Matters outcomes.

Children and young people make up 20 per cent of the population in England, which is equal to 11 million children and young people having a right to be heard. Just over three-quarters (77 per cent) of children and young people, according to MORI research conducted for 11 MILLION in 2006, were unaware of the United Nations Convention on the Rights of the Child. Clearly, much still needs to be done to ensure pupils are aware of their rights, and are involved more authentically in decision making related to their learning, well-being and school life in general. It is important that staff in schools and other educational settings communicate a genuine interest in what pupils have to say; learn to listen to their views; offer constructive and positive feedback to pupils, discussing lines of action and explaining why certain responses and actions may not be possible.

Improving schools listen to the views of their pupils, and pupils in those schools achieve best when their views, ideas and efforts are valued by adults. Children and young people, as partners and co-participants with adults in transforming school and local community change, want to know that their views have made a real difference in leading to change for the better. Children and young people, however, are a diverse group and these differences have an influence on the level of pupils' participation, voice and choice in a school. Schools therefore need to think creatively about the range of ways of gathering pupils' views, relaying information, and offering explanations to them, in order to ensure all pupils, including those with learning difficulties and disabilities, are active participants in decision-making processes.

There is no blueprint as to how pupil voice can best be secured, heard and acted upon. Schools need to have the freedom to determine what their pupil voice provision will entail. The Parliamentary Under-Secretary of State for Schools and Learners, Lord Andrew Adonis commented:

> Schools vary hugely across the country. This diversity means that we do not think it suitable to be prescriptive on how they encourage their pupils' participation to suit their differing needs and circumstances.

(Stewart 2007)

What is important for all schools is that they link their pupil voice provision to planning around Every Child Matters. Having a whole school pupil voice policy that reflects a set of commonly agreed values, and which offers a clear rationale for guiding the school's work in this aspect, as well as evaluating its success and impact regularly, is crucial in helping staff to understand why it is worthwhile engaging with pupil voice.

This book offers those working directly with children and young people in schools, and in other educational settings:

- an insight into the origins of pupil voice and children's rights;

- clarification of pupil voice terminology;
- a range of practical approaches and models of good practice in gathering pupils' views and ideas at whole school and classroom level, in relation to Every Child Matters;
- useful tools to evaluate the impact and outcomes of engaging pupils' voice and participation, from an adult and pupils' perspective;
- signposting to further sources of information.

Every child's views matter; the voice of the pupil should not be ignored.

Cullingford commented:

> Children's views deserve to be taken into account because they know better than anyone which teaching and learning styles are successful, which techniques of learning bring the best out of them and what the ethos of the school consists of . . . listening to children makes us consider some of the habits we have taken for granted.
>
> (Cullingford 1991: 2)

Overall, this valuable and ground-breaking resource brings together in one volume all the essential information necessary to ensure that pupil voice is encouraged, enhanced and empowered. Enjoy using the book to achieve the ultimate goal of securing better outcomes for children and young people.

1

The Origin and Concept of Pupil Voice

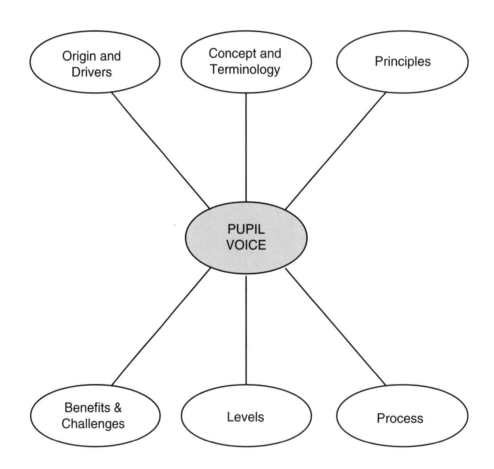

This chapter provides a comprehensive overview of the origin, concept, principles, benefits and challenges, process and levels of pupil voice and participation, without being too technical. Such an overview is particularly valuable to enable any professional from education, health and social care, working directly with children and young people in a range of educational settings, to transfer and apply the basic theory of pupil voice to the practical situation, at whole school, and classroom level. Further activities at the end of the chapter, which are solution focused, are offered to allow for reflection and analysis.

The origin of pupil voice

The origin and development of pupil voice has its roots predominantly in the twentieth century. Children in the nineteenth century were considered to be passive, silent, compliant, submissive and incompetent spectators in life events. They were to be seen and not heard, and were under the control and surveillance of either their parents or legal guardians; or the State and Victorian philanthropists, if they were vulnerable orphans, illegitimate or ineducable. Many working-class children at this time were exploited by unscrupulous employers in factories. Some were vulnerable to sexual exploitation, and many were affected by war and its aftermath.

While Chapter 2 looks in more detail at the rights of children and young people, there was clearly one key development in the latter half of the twentieth century that began to advocate the voice of the child. This was Articles 12 and 13 of the United Nations Convention on the Rights of the Child (UNCRC) in 1989, which stated:

> States Parties shall assure to the child who is capable of forming his or her own views the right to express those views freely, in all matters affecting the child, the views of the child being given due weight in accordance with the age and maturity of the child.
>
> (UNCRC 1989, Article 12: 1)

> The child shall have the right to freedom of expression; this right shall include freedom to seek, receive and impart information and ideas of all kinds . . . either orally, in writing or in print, in the form of art, or through any other media of the child's choice.
>
> (UNCRC 1989, Article 13: 1)

These two Articles of the UNCRC provide the initial justification as to why anyone working with children and young people should encourage and take notice of pupil voice, in whatever form it takes.

In the UK, developments related to pupils having a say in matters that affect their lives has largely been welfarist, and apparent in the legal, medical and social work fields, rather than in education. Some teachers in the past have underestimated the power of pupil voice, by making decisions on pupils' behalf related to their learning and school life in general.

The more recent personalisation and Every Child Matters agendas in the twenty-first century are beginning to change this situation, by ensuring that pupils' needs are central to everything that is done by educational settings and children's services, and that their views inform provision and service delivery.

The concept of pupil voice

Pupil voice can mean very different things to various people. According to Michael Fielding (2004), pupil voice can be a misleading concept because of pupil diversity, i.e. it is not fixed and absolute, but constantly changing and evolving in dialogue. For example, not all pupils necessarily share the same views as those who speak out. Some pupils' voices are more willing to speak out than others. Some pupils may not express ideas, views or opinions in acceptable ways to adults. There may be a lack of consensus as different subgroups of pupils take a different stance on an issue such as Every Child Matters.

Pupil voice in its widest sense can be defined as every way in which pupils are allowed or encouraged to voice their views or preferences. Taken more narrowly, in a nutshell, pupil voice can be understood as pupils having the opportunity to have a say in decisions in school that affect them. It entails pupils playing an active role in their education and schooling as a result of schools becoming more attentive and responsive, in sustained and routine ways, to pupils' views.

The term pupil voice can usefully be extended to include taking an active interest in events and developing a positive sense of belonging. The National Healthy School Standard (NHSS) stated:

> Giving pupils a voice means making it part of normal school practices for them to have a real say in what happens within the school, and real opportunity to take part.
>
> (DfES 2004c)

Pupil voice is the individual and collective perspectives and actions of children and young people within the context of learning and education, according to Adam Fletcher, a leading expert in the aspect. This can include, but is not limited to active or passive participation, knowledge, voting, wisdom, activism, service, and leadership.

Pupil voice reflects identity and is formed in the same ways as that of the adult voice, i.e. through experience, knowledge and education which help pupils like adults, to create opinions, ideas and beliefs, to which they give their voice. It is important, however, to remember that the voice of pupils, teachers and other adults working in an educational setting must be acknowledged and valued equally.

Pupil voice should not be interpreted exclusively in a narrow way to promote using pupils as issue-specific sounding boards. Pupil voice should allow children and young people to share who they are, what they believe, and why they believe what they do with their peers, parents/carers, teachers and other supportive adults, and their entire school.

Although pupil voice as a term is often used synonymously with engagement, involvement, participation and consultation, in research reports and government documentation, Adam Fletcher considers pupil voice is not the same.

Engagement is the excitement and investment a pupil feels towards an aspect or issue that interests them. Pupils are inspired and enthused by the belief that their ideas matter and will make a difference.

Involvement is the process of engaging pupils as partners in school improvement for the purpose of strengthening their commitment to education, community or democracy.

Participation is the self-determined act of pupils committing to something worthwhile in school, the community or society as a whole. Pupil participation, according to the DfES, means:

> . . . opening up opportunities for decision-making with children and young people as partners engaging in dialogue, conflict resolution, negotiation and compromise – all important life skills . . .
>
> (2004b: 2)

Pupil participation, according to Hugh Matthews (2001), assumes an ability to influence and change. It provides pupils with the opportunity to think for themselves and interact with others in a positive way.

Consultation is the systematic process of listening to pupils' opinions on an issue or topic such as Every Child Matters. It is about talking with pupils about things that matter in an educational setting, and seeking their advice and evaluative comments about particular initiatives.

The principles of pupil voice

The principles of pupil voice need to penetrate every aspect of an educational setting's organisation and operation, according to Kaye Johnson (2004). The key principles in relation to pupil voice activities at whole school and classroom level are:

- mutual respect is given and received between adults and pupils;
- pupils have equal value and worth to adults in school;
- communication is open, honest and valued and provides an exchange of ideas and views between pupils and staff;
- investment in the future, accepting that pupils are entitled to express their views about things that will affect and determine their future;
- meaningful active involvement where any decisions about pupils are made with them;
- teacher–pupil relationships are sustainable and responsive;
- equal opportunities exist for pupils to be involved in a range of pupil voice activities, e.g. younger and older pupils make equal contributions;
- pupils' participation, involvement and voice are continually evaluated and reviewed.

Drivers for engaging pupil voice

There are four main drivers which provide a good basis for considering the aims and objectives for provision for pupil voice. Table 1.1 summarises the main features of each driver.

Types of pupil voice

There are three main types of pupil voice:

1 **Authoritative voice** – representative of a particular group of pupils in a school, e.g. gifted and talented pupils
2 **Critical voice** – targeted at a particular pupil audience such as vulnerable children and young people to inform service provision
3 **Therapeutic voice** – emphatic voice expressed in dialogue between pupils that validates the experiences of pupils by reflecting on issues and problems, e.g. peer mentoring and peer counselling.

Categories of pupil voice activities

Michael Fielding (2004) usefully identified three broad categories through which to understand the different approaches to pupil voice and these are shown in Table 1.2.

Benefits of pupil voice

There are many benefits to engaging pupil voice for pupils and teachers. The main benefits are as follows:

- gives the teacher and other supportive adults additional information and an insight into what pupils think;
- helps to strengthen partnerships between pupils and teachers;
- helps adults to work out what is best for pupils;

Table 1.1 Drivers for engaging pupil voice

Driver	Features
Children's rights – recognition of rights, including the right to have their opinions taken into account in decisions that concern them	■ Pupil voice provision is fully embedded in the school's decision-making structure ■ There are opportunities for all pupils to be involved in decision making ■ Training is provided to pupils to enable their effective participation in decision making
Active citizenship – highlights how pupil voice can contribute to preparation for citizenship by improving pupils' knowledge and social skills, and, in doing so, can enhance the quality of democracy	■ There are direct links to the citizenship curriculum ■ Formal and consistent arrangements exist across the school for the election of school council representatives ■ Regular school council meetings are held, with good communication channels to and from the whole school ■ There are opportunities for all pupils to benefit from training in relation to the school council
School improvement – recognises that consultation with pupils can lead to better school performance in relation to pupils' behaviour, engagement or attainment	■ There are formalised links to the senior leadership team ■ There is regular pupil involvement in teaching, learning and well-being developments and issues, including the appointment of staff ■ A good range of pupil voice activities are utilised throughout the whole school, to contribute to school self-evaluation
Personalisation – pupil voice is utilised to ensure that the school meets the specific needs of its pupils as consumers or co-producers of education. It establishes the habit of talking about learning, teaching and well-being, and how to improve these aspects.	■ There is pupil involvement in most areas of decision making in school ■ There is regular consultation with pupils on a class-by-class and individual basis in relation to learning and ECM well-being ■ Formal links exist between pupil voice activity and parents/carers and the local community

Source: Whitty and Wisby DCSF RR001 2007: 95

- enables teachers to gain a better understanding of the things that really matter to pupils;
- enables adults to see things from the pupils' perspective;
- helps to create a listening organisation;
- pupils feel valued, respected and treated like adults;
- helps to develop reflective thinking in teachers and pupils;
- helps pupils to recognise that they are taken seriously by adults, resulting in increased confidence, self-esteem and aspirations;
- enables pupils to become more motivated to get involved in the school and in the wider community;
- helps pupils to develop new skills such as debating, negotiating, group decision making, how to influence others;
- provides a more inclusive approach to school self-evaluation;

Table 1.2 Categories of pupil voice activities

Category of pupil voice activities	Examples of pupil voice activities
Peer support arrangements	▪ Buddying ▪ Peer mentoring ▪ Circle time ▪ Peer tutoring ▪ Peer counselling
Systems that enable pupils to articulate their views and see through appropriate changes	▪ School councils ▪ Working groups ▪ Citizens' juries ▪ Involvement in reviews ▪ Pupils as researchers ▪ Pupils as associate governors ▪ Pupils on appointment panels
Activities that encourage various forms of overt pupil leadership	▪ Pupils as lead learners ▪ Pupils leading learning walks

Source: Adapted from Fielding 2004: 199

- strengthens the feeling of belonging to the school community showing pupils that they really can make a difference to how things are done in school;
- increases pupils' understanding and ownership of their own learning and well-being;
- helps pupils to clarify their own wants and needs and to communicate these to adults in a meaningful way;
- helps to facilitate the personal development of pupils to enable them to take on new responsibilities and make a positive contribution;
- promotes greater respect for democratic ways of working between staff and pupils;
- promotes more creative thinking.

Challenges of pupil voice

Some of the challenges that adults and staff in schools may experience as a result of pupils having a greater voice and choice in school can be summarised as follows.

- Some staff in school may be anxious about pupil criticism of aspects of their work.
- Some teachers may be wary of the unpredictability of pupils' comments and views.
- Some staff in school may have reservations about pupils having a voice and choice.
- Staff, and particularly teachers, may worry about the increasing workload brought about by engaging more proactively with pupil voice.
- Teachers in particular may worry about the loss of authority and the change in the balance of power through giving pupils a greater voice in the classroom.
- Some staff may have a view that some pupils are too young and immature to be able to express a sensible view or opinion.
- Some teachers may lack the confidence and skills in engaging pupil voice.
- There may be a gap between the school leaders' vision for pupil voice and the reality of pupil voice in practice.

Checklist for effective pupil voice involvement

- Pupils are clear about what they are being consulted on
- Pupils know who is being consulted, e.g. all or a specific group
- Pupils know at which stage in the decision-making process they are being involved
- Pupils know how much power, say and influence they will have
- Appropriate methods are used to gather pupils' views
- Pupils fully understand the decision-making process in school
- Pupils are given feedback on their views and ideas
- Pupils are clear about the benefits of participating in pupil voice activities
- There are sufficient resources available for pupil voice activities
- There are appropriate environments in school for engaging pupil voice
- The risks and challenges of strengthening pupil voice are known
- There is a designated member of staff who coordinates and leads pupil voice activities across the school
- Good practice in pupil voice is disseminated and shared with other schools and educational settings

Popular themes for pupil voice activities

Table 1.3 outlines some of the popular themes covered by pupil voice at whole school, year group and at classroom level. It is useful to think how pupil voice, at each level, could be sought on Every Child Matters.

Table 1.3 Popular themes for pupil voice activities

Whole school issues	Year group issues	Classroom issues (teaching and learning)
■ Revising the school mission statement ■ Changing the rewards system ■ Revising the school rules ■ Strategies for minimising bullying ■ School uniform ■ Effective working of school council ■ Improving the school library/resource centre ■ Qualities needed in a new head teacher ■ Ways of giving each year group an identity	■ Planning a year group induction ■ Involving parents/carers ■ Qualities needed in a year tutor ■ What feedback helps pupils to improve their work ■ Target setting and what pupils think of this process ■ Year group responsibilities and special duties ■ Best ways of organising homework	■ Identifying things that help pupils learn ■ Identifying barriers to learning ■ Reducing classroom noise ■ What pupils would like more of in lessons ■ What pupils would like less of in lessons ■ Classroom seating arrangements for pupils ■ Different grouping arrangements for pupils in lessons ■ Peer support in learning ■ Best ways of starting and ending a lesson ■ Ways of catching up if pupils miss work

Source: Macbeath *et al.* 2003: 50–51

Pupil voice processes

The process of engaging pupil voice at whole school, or classroom level, is best explained by focusing on two models. The first is Adam Fletcher's cycle of meaningful pupil voice and involvement, and the second is Roger Hart's ladder of pupil participation.

Cycle of meaningful pupil voice involvement

The cycle illustrates the steps teachers should take to encourage pupil voice. Adam Fletcher conceived the five-step continuous cycle of meaningful pupil involvement after studying the operation of pupil voice activities across the USA. The cycle represents a common pattern of stages that occur in every meaningful pupil voice and involvement activity.

It is the connection of all the steps in the cycle that make partnerships between pupils and adults in school meaningful, effective and sustainable. By following the cycle of meaningful pupil involvement, pupil participation is transformed into a process of promoting pupil achievement and school improvement.

Teachers, and other practitioners working directly with pupils in school, can use the cycle to assess current pupil voice activities and plan for future pupil voice activities, particularly in relation to improving the Every Child Matters outcomes.

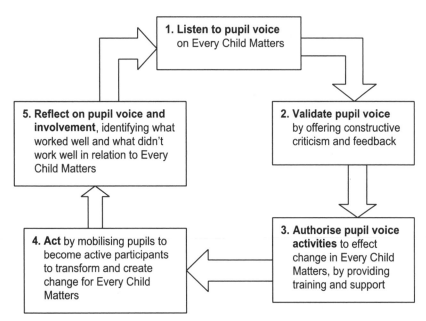

Figure 1.1 Cycle of meaningful pupil voice involvement. Source: Adam Fletcher 2004, *Meaningful Student Involvement: Guide to Students as Partners in School Change.*

Ladder of pupil participation

The ladder of pupil participation is a model developed by Roger Hart that depicts a continuum of ways pupils are involved in schools. Each rung on the ladder represents increased pupil empowerment and shared adult/pupil responsibility along the journey of participation from rung one to rung eight. The bottom three rungs of the ladder describe limited pupil involvement which is adult-led, while the top five rungs describe 'true' pupil participation that is child-initiated. The steps on the ladder illustrate and describe the degree to which pupils are in control of the process. Different levels on the ladder are appropriate for different pupil voice activities. The higher the rung on the ladder, the greater is the meaningfulness of pupil involvement.

Roger Hart's ladder of pupil participation can be used to measure and assess the levels of pupil participation, which includes pupil voice activities. The ladder offers a useful framework to help teachers and other staff to understand the different levels of pupil participation and empowerment. The ladder does not necessarily have to be followed sequentially or incrementally, as a school or class teacher may jump from the second rung to the sixth rung, according to the nature of the pupil voice activity. The ladder highlights that pupil participation can take various forms and different degrees, depending on the range of contextual factors at whole school and classroom level.

The ladder offers school leaders and class teachers a guide to the nature of pupil involvement and participation, as well as acting as point of reference to how the quality of pupil participation might be improved.

A class teacher or senior manager may use Hart's ladder in two ways:

1 To identify current levels of pupil participation
2 To identify future position in relation to further developing pupil participation.

Table 1.4 Ladder of pupil participation

Steps on the ladder	Features
8. **Pupil-initiated activities and shared decisions with adults**	Pupils are empowered and learn from the life experience and expertise of adults. Pupils identify or conceive the initial idea and then invite adults as equal partners to work in partnership with them. Pupils share power and responsibility for decision making with adults.
7. **Pupil-initiated, led and directed, pupil-centred decision making,** where adults are involved in only a supportive role	Both the original and initial ideas are derived from pupils, and focus on a pupil concern. The pupils decide how the project, initiative or activity is to be carried out. Pupils are fully involved in the decision-making process. Adults are available but do not take charge.
6. **Adult-initiated and directed,** where adult-led decision making is shared with pupils	Adults seek to involve pupils fully in the decision-making process. Although adults have the initial idea they do involve pupils in every step of the planning and implementation. Pupils' views are taken into account and considered, and they are involved in taking the decisions.
5. **Pupils consulted and informed** and where adult-led decision making is informed by pupil voice	Pupils give advice on activities, projects and initiatives designed and run by adults. Pupils are informed about how their input will be used and of the outcomes of the decisions made by adults. Pupils understand the process and their opinions are taken seriously. Pupils are supported in expressing their views.
4. **Assigned but informed participation** where pupils are assigned a specific role to respond to adult-led decision making, and are informed about how and why they are being involved	Pupils understand the activity, project or initiative and volunteer to participate, after the purpose has been made clear to them by adults in school. Pupils are listened to and they know who wants their participation, and why they are being involved. Adults respect pupils' views.

3. **Tokenism** where pupils appear to be given a voice by adults in the decision-making process, but in fact have little or no choice about what they do or how they participate	Although pupils appear to be given a voice, they have little or no choice about what they do, the subject pursued, the style of communication used, or how they participate, or any say in organising the event, activity.
2. **Decoration** where adults indirectly use pupils to help 'bolster' an adult identified cause, to decorate their decision making	Pupils are asked to take part in an activity but are not given any explanation of the issues or reasons for their involvement. Adults determine the cause and adults make all the decisions.

1. **Manipulation** where adults manipulate pupils in decision making and use them to support causes which adults want to pursue, pretending that the causes are inspired by pupils	Pupils do or say what adults in school wish them to do or say. Pupils have no real understanding of the issues.
	    Adults may use some of the pupils' ideas but do not tell them what influence these have had on final decisions made.
	    Adults pretend causes have been inspired by pupils.

Source: R. Hart, *Children's Participation: From Tokenism to Citizenship* (UNICEF, 1992)

Harry Shier's model framework of pathways to pupil participation (see Fig. 1.2 overleaf) maps loosely to Hart's ladder of participation, informing future pupil voice planning.

Further activities

The following questions, based on aspects covered in this chapter, are designed to enable you to discuss and identify positive ways forward, in meeting the challenges and opportunities in developing and engaging pupil voice, at whole school and classroom level.

- What is already being done in school to develop and improve pupil voice?
- What more could be done in school or in your classroom to further develop and improve pupil voice?
- How can you as a class teacher create a climate in which pupil voice can flourish?
- How can the senior leadership team ensure pupil voice is promoted consistently throughout the school?
- What more can school leaders do to help class teachers feel more confident about building pupil voice activities into their daily classroom practice?
- How can staff fears, uncertainty or anxieties about pupil voice be allayed?
- How can school leaders reassure staff, parents/carers and governors that pupil voice is a legitimate practice that supports Every Child Matters and citizenship education?
- How will you keep a healthy balance between individual pupil voice and collective pupil voice activities in personalised learning?
- How could you become more involved in seeking pupils' views?
- How could the school/classroom climate be more accommodating to pupil voice?
- At what position on Hart's ladder is your class currently at?
- How might you move your class to a higher position on Hart's ladder?

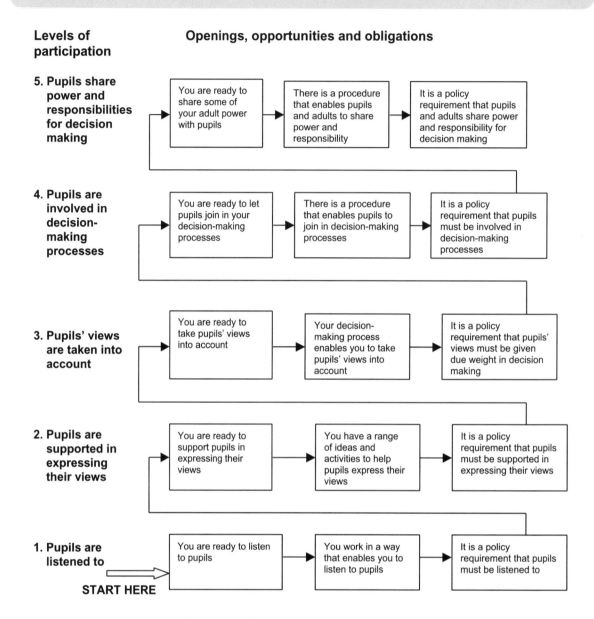

Figure 1.2 Framework of levels and pathways to pupil participation.* Source: Adapted from Harry Shier 2001, 'Pathways to participation'.

Note: *This model is applicable across a wide range of different settings, including the example of the formal school followed in this book.

2

The Rights of Children and Young People

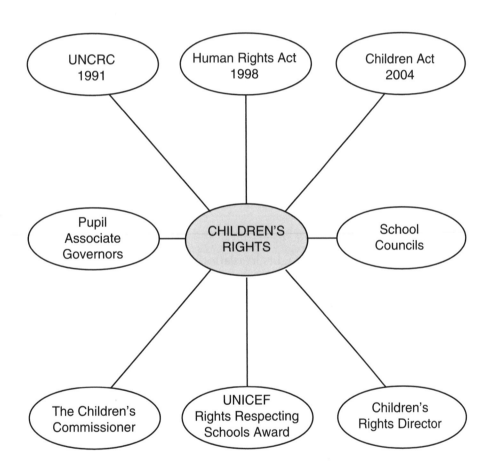

The children's rights movement developed and flourished in the twentieth century as a result of the desire of governments within the United Nations, which includes the UK, wishing to safeguard and protect the welfare of children and young people.

Maud de Boer-Buquicchio, Deputy Secretary General of the Council of Europe, in a speech in October 2005 commented:

> Children are not mini-persons with mini-rights, mini-feelings and mini-human dignity. They are vulnerable human beings with full rights that require more, not less protection.

Children, like any adult, have the basic human rights to be treated with dignity, fairness, equality, respect and autonomy, in order to fulfil their potential. All children and young people have over forty rights that say how they can be expected to be treated by others – at home, at school, or in their neighbourhood.

This chapter provides a comprehensive, user-friendly guide to all the relevant legislation pertaining to pupil voice, applicable to England. This enables the practitioner to have a secure point of reference on which to base and justify any activities and developments that engage and enhance pupil voice in schools, and other educational settings. A brief overview is also provided on the role of the school council, pupil associate governors, the Children's Rights Director, and the Children's Commissioner for England. The chapter concludes with further activities that raise a series of questions on pupils' rights, which merit further exploration, at a whole school, and classroom level.

Children and young people's rights and the law

Table 2.1 provides an 'at-a-glance' guide to the most significant and relevant legislation pertaining to all children's rights and pupil voice.

Table 2.1 Children and young people's rights legislation

Children's rights legislation	Features of the children's rights legislation
Universal Declaration of Human Rights 1948	Adopted 10 December 1948 and comprised 30 Articles. All member countries to publicise the text of the Declaration and to cause it to be disseminated, displayed, read and expounded principally in schools and other educational institutions. The Declaration revived an interest in children's rights. **Article 19** – Everyone has the right to freedom of opinion and expression; this right includes freedom to hold opinions without interference and to seek, receive and impart information and ideas through any media and regardless of frontiers. **Article 25(2)** – All children, whether born in or out of wedlock, shall enjoy the same social protection. **Article 26(3)** – Parents have a prior right to choose the kind of education that shall be given to their children.
The Declaration on the Rights of the Child 1959	Focus was largely on safeguarding and protecting children rather than on empowering them. It emphasised children's emotional well-being, i.e. the child's need for love, understanding and to grow up in an atmosphere of affection. It emphasised the priority and entitlement of children to emergency assistance, i.e. the child shall in all circumstances be among the first to receive protection and relief. It emphasised the rights and maintenance of the rights of the child.

	It emphasised the key role of parents, men and women, voluntary organisations, LAs and national governments in recognising and observing children's rights.
Children Act 1989	Implemented in 1991, the Act made it a legal requirement for children and young people to be consulted and involved in decisions that affected them. The implementation of the Act coincided with the UK ratification of the UNCRC in December 1991. Part 1 3a of the Act requires that whenever a court considers any question with respect to the welfare of a child, it must have regard to the ascertainable wishes and feelings of the child concerned (considered in the light of his/her age and understanding).
United Nations Convention on the Rights of the Child 1989	The UNCRC came into force on 2 September 1990, and was ratified in December 1991 in the UK. (The UK will be examined by the Geneva Committee on the Rights of the Child in 2009, to check if it is continuing to put the UNCRC into practice, see www.getreadyforgeneva.org.uk) This human rights treaty applies to every child and young person aged 17 and under. Only two countries, Somalia and the United States, did not ratify the UNCRC; (192 States out of 194 accepted the UNCRC). There are a total of 54 Articles of which 40 give direct rights to all children and young people. The Convention does not actually have direct legal effect within the UK, but it represents a benchmark for the UK law and government policy to note. **Article 2** – all the rights in the Convention apply to every child without discrimination. **Article 4** – the State has a duty to fully implement civil rights. **Article 5** – States must respect the rights and duties of parents/carers to provide, in a manner consistent with the evolving capacities of the child, appropriate direction and guidance relating to the rights in the convention. **Article 12** – the child's right to express and have his or her views given due weight in all matters affecting them. The child should be heard in any judicial and administrative proceeding. **Article 13** – the child's right to freedom of expression – to seek, receive and impart information orally, in writing or in print, in art form or through any other media of the child's choice. **Article 14** – the child's right to freedom of thought, conscience and religion. States shall respect the rights and duties of parents and legal guardians, to provide direction to the child in the exercise of his or her right in a manner consistent with the evolving capacities of the child. **Article 15** – the child's right to freedom of association and to peaceful assembly. **Article 16** – the child's right to protection from interference with his or her privacy, family, home or correspondence, and to protection from unlawful attacks on his or her honour and reputation. **Article 17** – the child's right to access information from national and international sources, especially those aimed at the promotion of his or her social, spiritual and moral well-being and physical and mental health. **Article 23** – disabled children's right to social integration and active participation in the community. **Article 29** – education must develop the child's personality, talents and mental and physical abilities to their fullest potential.

Table 2.1 (continued)

Children's rights legislation	Features of the children's rights legislation
	Article 30 – the child's right to enjoy his or her own culture, religion and language. **Article 31** – the child's right to rest and leisure and to play and recreation and to participate freely in cultural life and the arts. **Article 37** – every child deprived of his or her liberty has the right to prompt legal advice or other assistance. **Article 39** – States must promote the recovery and social reintegration of children who have been neglected, exploited or abused, or tortured or subject to any other cruel, inhuman or degrading treatment or punishment. Such measures should encourage the health, self-respect and dignity of the child. **Article 40** – the child's right to have legal or other appropriate assistance when he or she has been accused of or found to have committed a criminal offence. **Article 42** – States must inform adults and children alike about all the rights of children in the UNCRC, particularly those working with children, e.g. teachers, social workers, nurses.
Human Rights Act 1998	The Act incorporated the European Convention on Human Rights (ECHR) into domestic law. It came into force in England and Wales in October 2000. It enables UK citizens, which includes children and young people, to seek to protect their European Convention on Human Rights through domestic courts. In addition, they can still seek protection through the European Court of Human Rights in Strasbourg. The ECHR contains rights that are mainly civil and political. There are 13 substantive rights in the ECHR (articles 2 to 14). **Article 2** – the right to life **Article 3** – protection from torture or inhuman or degrading treatment or punishment **Article 4** – protection from slavery **Article 5** – right to liberty and security **Article 6** – the right to a fair trial, including the child's right to be informed promptly in a language he or she understands, of the alleged offence and to have an interpreter in court if he or she cannot understand or speak the language in court **Article 7** – no one can be punished for an act that was not a criminal offence when it was carried out **Article 8** – the right to respect for private and family life, home and correspondence **Article 9** – the right to freedom of thought, conscience and religion **Article 10** – the right to freedom of expression, to hold opinions and to receive and impart information and ideas without interference by public authorities and regardless of frontiers. The exercise of these freedoms may be subject to such formalities, conditions, restrictions or penalties as are prescribed by law and are necessary in a democratic society, in the interests of national security, public safety, for the prevention of disorder or crime, for the protection of health or morals, for the protection of the reputation of rights of others, for preventing the disclosure of information received in confidence, or for maintaining the authority and impartiality of the judiciary **Article 11** – the right to freedom of assembly and association

	Article 12 – right to marry **Article 13** – right to an effective remedy **Article 14** – all the rights in the Convention apply to all people without discrimination.
Education Act 2002	Part 11 Section 176 Consultation with Pupils, requires local education authorities and governing bodies to have regard to any guidance given by the Secretary of State on pupil consultation, in connection with the taking of decisions affecting them. This includes PRUs, but excludes nursery education. Any guidance under this section must provide for a pupil's views to be considered in the light of his or her age and understanding. It is, however, for LAs, teachers and governors to decide how best to involve children and young people. The DfES issued guidance in April 2004 entitled: *Working together: Giving children and young people a say.*

Children Act 2004	**Sections 1–9** provided for the creation of the Children's Commissioner for England and clarified the role of the Commissioner. In delivering the interests of children, the Commissioner must have regard to the UNCRC. He must publish reports in child-friendly versions for children and young people.
	Section 10 requires Children's Services authorities and their partners to cooperate to improve the well-being of children in their area, particularly in the aspect of the contribution made by them to society. It stipulates that local children's services should reflect the needs of children and young people and that, accordingly, local authorities and partners need to encourage a good level of participation by children and young people in the design and delivery of services.
	Section 17 requires children and young people to be consulted in the preparation of the local authority Children and Young People's Plan, as their genuine participation is crucially important, along with that of parents, carers and families.
	Section 53 – *Ascertaining children's wishes*, amends the Children Act 1989 in two places:
	  ■ Children in need
	There is a new Section 17 (4A) duty on local authorities to, so far as is reasonably practicable and consistent with the child's welfare, ascertain the child's wishes and feelings regarding the provision of those services, and give them due consideration (having regard to the child's age and understanding).
	  ■ Child protection enquiries
	There is a new Section 47 (5A) duty on local authorities to, so far as is reasonably practicable and consistent with the child's welfare, ascertain the child's wishes and feelings regarding the action to be taken, and give them due consideration (having regard to the child's age and understanding).

For further information see Children's Rights Alliance for England (2007), *Ready Steady Change, Rights and the Law*

UNICEF (2006) provides an excellent 'user-friendly' two-page document which maps and aligns the Articles of the United Nations Convention on the Rights of the Child (UNCRC) with the five Every Child Matters outcomes. The publication entitled *Every Child Matters. The five Outcomes and the UN Convention on the Rights of the Child (UNCRC)* can be downloaded free from the website: www.unicef.org.uk/tz/resources/assets/pdf/join_up_ecm_uncrc.pdf. The document provides a good point of reference for all those working directly with pupils in school, and in other educational settings.

The government's Children's Plan (DCSF 2007c), in *Annex B: The Children's Plan and the UNCRC*, aligns the Articles of the UN Convention on the Rights of the Child (UNCRC) against each key area/chapter of the Children's Plan. The full Children's Plan with Annexes can be accessed at the following website: www.dcsf.gov.uk/publications/childrensplan.

The government (DCSF 2007b) in Annex A of their publication entitled: *Children and Young People Today: Evidence to support the development of the Children's Plan* – which can be accessed and downloaded from the website: www.dcsf.gov.uk/timetotalk – maps the government's progress in relation to improving children and young people's well-being against the five Every Child Matters outcomes, to indicate good progress and areas where more work is required. This document may be of particular interest to school leaders, particularly those who are providing the full core offer of extended school services.

School councils

School councils have been in existence for almost forty years, with the first being introduced in the 1970s. Ireland, Germany, Spain and Sweden have to have a school council in every state secondary school. Their purpose is to involve pupils in the life of their school. They provide a formal structure which facilitates pupil–adult communication, and which enables pupils to take responsibility for aspects of school life that directly affect them.

A school council is defined as a democratically elected body of pupils whose purpose is to represent their classes of peers and to be a forum for active and constructive pupil input and positive contributions to the daily life of the school community.

School council, as an inclusive term, is also used for other similar pupil representative bodies such as School Parliament, Pupil/Student Council, or School Forum.

School councils provide an excellent vehicle for their members to learn about citizenship, democracy and local politics. The Education Act 2002 gave the government powers to prescribe regulations for school councils by order, but these were encouraged in England and not prescribed, unlike in Wales where it has been compulsory for every primary, secondary and special school to have a school council since December 2005.

The government in England, however, does recognise the value and the importance of school councils, but is not forcing every school to have one. Whitty and Wisby, in their research report on schools' councils (2007), found that 95 per cent of schools in England had a school council, but of these, one in ten were not hugely effective, and merely 'talking shops'. The three most common topics for discussion in secondary school councils were facilities, meals and uniform, and in primary school councils, playground issues were the top discussion topic.

School councils are of course only one component of overall pupil voice provision. They are an effective way of enabling pupils to exercise their rights under Article 12 of the United Nations Convention on the Rights of the Child. In relation to Every Child Matters (ECM) and pupils making a positive contribution, a school council could be divided into five working groups with each representing one of the five ECM outcomes. This would enable the school council to effect change in a far more focused way to improve ECM well-being outcomes for pupils in school.

Effective school councils have the following characteristics:

- feature in the School Prospectus, School Profile, school SEF, newsletters;
- have their own notice board in a prominent place in school, such as in the main entrance/reception area;

- are featured and have a link on the school's website;
- publicise agendas;
- post minutes promptly in all classrooms after meetings;
- hold purposeful meetings regularly, at least four every term;
- have a budget to manage;
- establish a clear rationale for involving pupil voice and evaluate its success regularly;
- have an agreed written constitution, which is clear about areas where there can be no pupil power;
- provide regular updates on progress in addressing pupils' issues raised through the school council;
- have continuity in membership, i.e. pupils serve at least one full year in office;
- provide training for school council members to undertake their respective roles;
- communicate and link with the school governing body.

Further information about school councils can be found on the School Councils UK website: www.schoolcouncils.org. The School Councils UK organisation was first formed in 1993.

Pupils as associate governors

Pupils under the age of 18 since 1 September 2003, under Statutory Guidance on the School Governance (Procedures) (England) Regulations 2003, Regulation 11, can become associate members of school governing bodies. Associate members are seen as a means of adding to the capacity of governing bodies, and in particular committees, by adding specific expertise on certain issues. For example, pupils as associate members may usefully offer advice and ideas from a pupil's perspective, representing pupils' views at governing body full meetings or committees. This helps governors to gain a real insight into pupils' thinking.

It is not compulsory for governing bodies to make appointments of pupil associate members, and such a decision rests with each school's governing body. Pupils as associate members are not part of the body corporate because they are under 18, which means that they are not legally responsible for the school as adult governors are. The governing body of a school has to agree to appoint pupil associate members and has to reconstitute to include them. Some schools may choose to appoint the Chair of the School Council as the pupil associate governor, as they already have the necessary skills to undertake the role. Pupil associate members of school governing bodies need to be skilled in participation and relaying information between staff, pupils and governors. They benefit from training for the role that covers: meeting structures, code of behaviour, negotiation skills, presenting a persuasive argument, confidentiality, and collective responsibility.

Pupil associate members work with the governing body to support and develop all areas of the school, and are considered to be at the heart of school decision making. However, they are not allowed to vote on decisions relating to admissions; the appointment of governors; pupil discipline; or the budget and financial commitments of the governing body. Associate members of the governing body can hold office for up to four years.

The Children's Rights Director

The Care Standards Act 2000, Schedule 1(10) first provided for the creation of the Children's Rights Director. However, Dr Roger Morgan, OBE, the first Children's Rights Director (CRD) for England and his team of five staff were not established until 2004, under the Commission for Social Care Inspection (Children's Rights Director) Regulations 2004. His legal duties are set out in the Office for Standards in Education, Children's Services and Skills (Children's Rights Director) Regulations 2007. He and his team relocated to OFSTED's Alexandra House in London in April 2007, from Newcastle.

The functions of the Children's Rights Director are:

- to advise and assist the Chief Inspector (OFSTED) when performing his/her functions
- safeguard and promote the rights and welfare of children
- have regard to the views expressed by children and young people about activities within their remit.

The Children's Rights Director's key role is to seek and listen to the views of looked after and vulnerable children and young people, and identify issues about their rights and welfare. He is particularly interested in the care of children and young people who are living away from home, who live in children's homes, boarding schools, residential special schools, residential FE colleges, foster care, residential family centres, children in adoption placements, and care leavers.

The Children's Rights Director for England conveys the views and concerns of these vulnerable children and young people, about the care and support they receive, to the Government, OFSTED, each of the UK's four Children's Commissioners, and to all children's social care authorities in England. Since the Children's Rights Director has been in post there have been a series of 26 Children's Views reports published, which can be viewed and downloaded from the OFSTED website and from the Children's Rights website: www.rights4me.org

In March 2007, the Commission for Social Care Inspection (CSCi) published *Policy by Children. A Children's Views Report* (2007). This report brought together all the ideas vulnerable children and young people had given to the Children's Rights Director and his team from 2004 to 2007, in the form of 107 policies that children and young people want people providing services to follow. In relation to children and young people's rights and voice, Policy 12 in the report states:

> Regularly ask children for their views and concerns, give children ways of saying their views and concerns at all times, take what they say as seriously as what adults say, take what they say into account in making decisions that affect children, and tell children what can or cannot happen in light of their views, and why.
>
> (CSCi 2007: 13)

Policy 41 in the report in relation to younger children's views on Every Child Matters states:

> In addition to the 'Every Child Matters' five outcomes of staying safe, being healthy, enjoying life and learning, helping others and having enough money, should be added the seven further priority outcomes identified by children: family, friends, food and drink, fun, love, respect and being happy. Making up a 'children's dozen' outcomes.
>
> (CSCi 2007: 24)

Policy 90 in the report states in relation to rights and responsibilities:

> Children should always receive feedback on what has been done with views they have given about important issues in their lives and future, and should always be given reasons for decisions and actions, including the reasons for deciding in a way that goes against their wishes.
>
> (CSCi 2007: 43)

The Children's Rights Director respects looked-after and vulnerable children and young people's right to privacy, confidentiality, information, to complain, and to have a say in giving their views.

The Office of the Children's Rights Director will be seeking the views of children and young people in relation to how the UK is doing on the United Nations Convention on the Rights of the Child during 2008.

The Children's Commissioner for England

The first Children's Commissioner for England, Sir Albert Aynsley Green was appointed in March 2005, and became fully operational on 1 July 2005. Wales has had a Children's Commissioner since 2000. Northern Ireland has had one since 2003, and Scotland appointed their Children's Commissioner in 2004.

Sections 1 to 9 of the Children Act 2004 provided for the creation of the Children's Commissioner for England and specified the role. The role of the Children's Commissioner in England is to:

- act as a national, independent voice for children and young people;
- promote awareness of views, needs, rights and interests of children and young people;
- raise the profile of children and young people in society;
- improve the lives and well-being of children and young people;
- encourage all those in the children's workforce, and those with responsibility for children, to take account of children and young people's views and interests;
- have regard to the United Nations Convention on the Rights of the Child (UNCRC) when determining what constitutes the interests of children and young people; and
- research issues that matter to children and young people, particularly those which no one else is dealing with.

The Children's Commissioner in England is committed to four fundamental underpinning principles of openness, honesty, transparency and ownership. The Children's Commissioner in England wants to see a society where children and young people:

1   are valued, are expected to make a contribution to society and are supported in doing so;
2   are truly at the centre of policy and practice;
3   have their views actively sought, listened to and acted upon;
4   have their rights upheld.

The Children's Commissioner's vision and mission are very clear.

VISION

Children and young people will actively be involved in shaping all decisions that affect their lives, are supported to achieve their full potential through the provision of appropriate services, and will live in homes and communities where their rights are respected and they are loved, safe and enjoy life.

MISSION

We will use our powers and independence to ensure that the views of children and young people are routinely asked for, listened to and acted upon and that outcomes for children improve over time. We will do this, in partnership with others, by bringing children and young people into the heart of the decision-making process to increase understanding of their best interests.

The Children's Commissioner for England holds a Big Discussion with children and young people every year in August. At this event children and young people agree the priorities for the coming year, and decide how 50 per cent of the Commissioner's project budget will be spent.

The Children's Commissioner in England launched a new strategy entitled '11 MILLION' on 16 May 2007, which explores six fundamental areas of concern regarding children's rights and well-being, which are: youth justice and anti-social behaviour; asylum and trafficking; a fair life; mental health; enjoying education and leisure; and, staying safe.

11 MILLION is also working to ensure that adults respect the rights of children and young people, and that every child knows about their rights. The Children's Commissioner in England launched the first 11 MILLION Takeover Day on Friday 23 November 2007. The aim of the day was to give some of England's 11 MILLION children and young people a taste of power in schools, businesses and politics by taking over adults' jobs.

The Children's Commissioner for England has a website: www.childrenscommissioner.org. Further information about his 11 MILLION initiative can be found at: www.11MILLION.org.uk

The UNICEF Rights Respecting Schools Award

This award scheme was launched in the UK in spring 2007, with 30 schools initially involved in piloting the award. The award scheme promotes the United Nations Convention on the Rights of the Child (UNCRC) as the basis for enhancing teaching, learning, ethos, attitudes and behaviour. The nationwide award scheme is open to all schools, e.g. nursery, primary, middle, secondary and special.

In order that a school receives the Rights Respecting Schools Award, they have to show evidence that they have reached the required standard in all four aspects which are:

1 Leadership and management for embedding the values of the UNCRC in the life of the school
2 Knowledge and understanding of the UNCRC
3 Rights respecting classrooms
4 Pupils actively participate in decision making throughout the school.

The award programme complements other schemes such as the Healthy Schools Award, ECO Schools Award, Basic Skills Award, the Inclusion Quality Mark, and the ECM Standards Award.

Schools that successfully meet the UNICEF Rights Respecting Schools criteria will receive a Rights Respecting Schools Award Certificate and digital logo.

There is a dedicated website that provides access to information and resources which individuals, schools, HE colleges and local authorities can utilise when they sign up to undertake the award.

Further information about the UNICEF Rights Respecting Schools Award can be found at: www.unicef.org.uk/tz/teacher_support/rrs_award.asp.

The Children's Society Good Childhood inquiry into learning stated:

> Adults need to understand that children can form and express their views in coherent and highly perceptive ways. . . . We must continue to promote participation as a right and not as a gift.

(2007c: 7)

Further activities

The following questions, based on aspects covered in this chapter, are designed to enable you to discuss and identify positive ways forward, in meeting the challenges and opportunities posed by embedding pupils' rights at whole school and classroom level.

- How have you informed pupils about their rights?
- Do the rights and participation agendas appeal to all pupils, or to only some more vocal groups? If this is the case, what action will you take to resolve the issue?
- Are you satisfied that all pupils have the opportunity to have a say and be involved in decision making within the school?
- What more could be done for the 'hard to reach' groups of pupils, in order to ensure that they know their rights and have a voice?
- How can you avoid diluting the significance of children's rights by embedding it in only the PSHE and citizenship curriculum?
- What responsibilities do teachers and other adults supporting children in school have in helping pupils to cope if sensitive issues arise when discussing rights?
- Where is the line drawn by adults/school staff in relation to empowering pupils' rights, voice and participation in decision making?
- How have you prepared teaching and support staff for understanding and acknowledging pupil rights in their daily practice?
- In what ways has the school council had an opportunity to discuss and address issues relating to the Every Child Matters agenda?
- How influential is your school council? How do you know?
- What more could be done to strengthen the role of the school council?
- How many pupils do you want to be associate members on the school governing body, as there is no minimum or maximum number specified?
- How long a term of office do you want pupil associate members to serve on the governing body? (One or two years, or more?)
- Do you want pupil associate members to serve on the full governing body, on committees, or both?
- How will you select, elect and appoint pupil associate members?
- Which year groups/key stages will pupil associate members come from?
- How will the associate members on the governing body link with and feedback to the school council?
- What training, support and accreditation will you provide for pupil associate members?
- How will you inform and prepare adults on the governing body for accepting and welcoming pupils as associate members?
- How will you ensure that pupil associate governors remain in touch with, connected to, and representative of the wider pupil body?

- Are there any pitfalls of associate membership for pupils themselves, or for the wider governing body?
- If there are likely to be pitfalls, how do you intend to respond to, or pre-empt these?
- Do the advantages of pupil associate members on the governing body outweigh the disadvantages?

3

Key National Surveys and Reports Engaging Pupil Voice

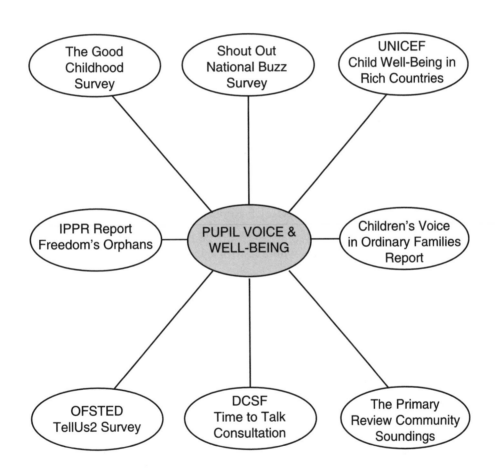

The opening years of the twenty-first century have brought a plethora of surveys and reports, arising as a result of the government and other organisations undertaking national consultations with children and young people.

As early as 2002, prior to the publication of the Green Paper *Every Child Matters* in 2003, BT undertook a national research project entitled Are Young People Being Heard? They found that fewer than half of the young people in the UK at that time felt that their voices were being listened to and acted upon.

Similarly, only 53 per cent of adults agreed that they listened to and acted upon what they heard from young people. Both adults and young people agreed that listening to each other more would help them understand each other better. The lack of time was cited by adults as the main reason as to why they were too busy to listen to young people. The DCSF (2007a) in their recent 'Time to Talk' community consultation also discovered that parents worried about not spending enough time with their children, due to the pressures of work.

What all the recent key national surveys and reports appear to focus on is the well-being of children and young people, particularly in relation to the five Every Child Matters outcomes. The recent frenzied activity at taking a closer look into children and young people's experiences of growing up and living in a society where childhood innocence appears to be lost to the adverse pressures of a cocktail of toxic childhood factors such as junk food diets, couch potato passive technological lifestyles, stranger danger play limitations, excessive consumerism, the glorification of a celebrity culture and a narrow test-and-target driven curriculum, indicates the urgent need for the government to greatly improve the current situation in England.

It was a revelation to discover from the UNICEF Report on Child Well-Being in Rich Countries (2007a), that one of the worst places for a child or young person's well-being was the UK, which came 21st out of a total of 25 countries, where Estonia, Latvia, Lithuania and Slovakia were the lowest.

Tables 3.1 and 3.2 provide a comprehensive overview of the most significant and telling national surveys and reports published between 2006 and 2007, which sought and focused on pupil voice. While the findings and recommendations from each survey and report make for interesting reading, they raise two initial crucial questions for the reader to reflect on in relation to the situation in their own educational context.

1 How do the findings from each national survey and report reflect the current situation in the educational setting you are working in?
2 How can the findings and recommendations from these national surveys and reports be utilised to improve the Every Child Matters well-being outcomes for pupils in your school, and more importantly in your everyday work with pupils?

The Howard League for Penal Reform commented in its report on child crime in October 2007:

> If the government strategy on engaging young people and vulnerable groups is to be effective, it needs to ensure that it is talking with, listening to and engaging all children, to guarantee that the correct services are being provided for them.
>
> (Howard League 2007b: 2)

Clearly, many of the recent national surveys have been related to consultation in seeking the views of children and young people, rather than involving them more proactively in the actual decision-making process.

Table 3.1 National Surveys and Pupil Voice

4Children My Shout Out! National Buzz Survey	OFSTED TellUs2 Survey
Background The national charity 4Children undertook a national survey seeking the views of children and young people about issues that concern them and who can help to make the world a better place for children. 1,000 children aged 4 to 14 participated in the survey, of which 48% were boys and 52% were girls. The findings from the survey were published in June 2007. **Key findings** **Things children worry about** 78% bullying; 76% war; 75% the environment and child poverty; 72% racism, terrorism and anti-social behaviour; 69% climate change; 54% turning down the heating. **People who inspire children** 77% mother; 67% father; 58% friends; 52% other family members; 45% grandparents; 42% teachers; 28% famous people living today; 23% play/youth worker; 21% people from history **Who does a lot to make the children's world better** 59% God; 52% Tony Blair; 27% Gordon Brown; 21% Wayne Rooney; 17% Christiano Ronaldo; 16% Ben 10; 13% Allah; 12% Lenny Henry; 11% Kylie Minogue and Nelson Mandela; 9% Bob Geldof; 8% Bill Gates and David Cameron; 7% Richard Branson; 4% Dalai Lama and Jade Goody **Things that would make children's lives better** 89% being kind to friends and family; 88% volunteering to help others; 87% recycling things; 84% giving money to charity; 83% being kind to neighbours; 81% not dropping litter; 79% using the car less and turning off the standby on the TV and computer; 78% turning the heating down and turning off the lights; 77% using less water; 76% no graffiti; 74% not dropping chewing gum; 70% praying **Changes children want to make to their lives** 30% want to behave better in some way to parents, friends and teachers 13% want to do something more positively environmentally friendly 78% want more support from school to make their lives and the world around them better 77% want more support from family and friends to make their lives and the world around them better	**Background** 111,325 children, aged between 10 and 15 in England, participated in the survey via schools, across 141 local authorities, during April to June 2007. The survey focused on the Every Child Matters well-being outcomes. **Key findings** 86% of children consider themselves to be quite or very healthy 73% of children participate in sports or other activities such as cycling and running for at least 30 minutes on more than 3 days a week 65% of children have helped to raise money for charity or for a local group 52% of Year 8 and Year 10 pupils feel that their views are listened to in the running of their school 55% of Year 8 and Year 10 pupils want more or better advice when planning their future 48% of all children between 10 and 15 claimed they had had an alcoholic drink 19% (1 in 5) children have been drunk at least once in the past four weeks 15% of children aged 12 to 15 have tried drugs 30% of children had been bullied at least a couple of times in the last month 31% of children want fewer bullies; 30% of children consider bullying is not handled or not handled very well 79% of pupils want more fun and interesting lessons at school; 40% want more help from teachers; 40% want quieter and better behaved classmates **Biggest worries on children's minds** 51% exams; 39% friendships; 35% school work; 32% being healthy; 30% their future. **Recommendations** ■ More needs to be done to address children's and young people's worries and concerns about how safe they feel; about exams and tests; about what would help them learn better, and where they need to go for help when they have a problem ■ The level of smoking, drinking and drug misuse among some young people needs addressing ■ More needs to be done to tackle bullying ■ There needs to be better advice on careers, sex and relationships Schools are advised by OFSTED to use the information from the TellUs2 survey to compare themselves with others in their area. OFSTED will undertake another TellUs3 Survey in 2008.

Table 3.1 Continued

The Children's Society – Good Childhood Inquiry	The Children's Society Good Childhood Thematic Surveys
Background Initial national survey of over 11,000 young people aged 14 to 16 in sixteen areas of England took place in 2005 and the findings were published in a launch report in July 2006. It explored what the conditions are for a good childhood, and what changes could be made to improve childhood. **Main findings: childhood in the UK today** 64% of children aged 8 to 15 have internet access at home 65% of children have their own mobile phone 29% of children & young people long for someone to turn to for advice 93% of young people felt their parents/carers cared about them 63% felt their parents/carers understood them 7% of young people were bullied and picked on because of who they were 24% of young people were sometimes bullied and picked on because of who they were 60% of young people often hang about with their friends doing nothing in particular 58% of young people were worried about their exams at school 47% said that they often worried about school work 8% considered they had an alcohol problem 5% considered they had a problem with drugs 49% considered that there were no places for young people to go in their area 75% of young people liked living in their area 18% of young people said that they did not feel safe when they were out alone in their local area 29% considered that violence was a growing problem in their area 36% of young people felt that gangs were a growing problem in their area 42% of young people did not consider that their area cared about young people 78% of young people find life really worth living 75% of young people felt their life had a sense of purpose A final report with recommendations will be published at the end of the inquiry in autumn 2008.	**Background** A series of six thematic surveys were undertaken during 2007 to 2008 which covered: friends; family; learning; lifestyle; health; and values. **Good childhood: friends** **Main findings** ■ From the age of 2 friendships are very important for children's well-being ■ Adults often underestimate the importance of friendship for children in helping them adjust to and cope with life experiences ■ Children experience deep unhappiness when separated from friends, which can result in poorer mental health ■ Parents intervene in a child's friendship when they are not happy with it ■ Children who have difficulty making and keeping friends feel isolated and depressed ■ Rejection by other children is consistently linked to problems such as depression, aggressive, anti-social and delinquent behaviour ■ The number of teenagers with no best friends has increased to one in five ■ There has been an increase in the number of 16-year-olds assaulted by a peer or threatened with violence ■ Having friends makes for a good childhood and happiness at school ■ The qualities children valued most in a friend were: trustworthiness, a sense of humour, kindness, supportiveness, and those similar to themselves ■ The qualities children dislike in a friend are when they are untrustworthy, selfish, unkind, 'bitchy', ignore them, make fun of them, or fall out with them ■ Children see friends as someone they can rely on, talk to about things that matter to them, and someone who will 'stick up' for them ■ Bullying is a major concern for children and young people, and they consider not enough is being done to address the problem ■ Homophobic bullying has become a significant issue for children and more needs to be done to tackle the issue ■ If children and young people need help with a problem, 46% would go to a friend and 35% would go to a parent

The Children's Society Good Childhood Thematic Surveys	The Children's Society Good Childhood Thematic Surveys
Good childhood: family	**Good childhood: learning**
Main findings	**Main findings**
<ul><li>Good relationships between parent and child can lead to positive outcomes for children which include: high achievement, greater social competence and good peer relationships</li><li>70% children and young people see love as the most important element of a good life, a happy family and a good parent</li><li>Children and young people consider feeling valued and having a supportive and caring family as being important</li><li>Children identify the attributes that make a good parent as being: love, support, care, fun and kindness, mutual respect and trust</li><li>Children and young people regard good parenting as including a respect for their freedom and independence</li><li>They dislike overprotective parents</li><li>Many children and young people value a happy family where there is good, open and supportive communication, where they can talk about and express significant issues and inner worries</li><li>Several children and young people considered their parents were too busy to spend time with them</li><li>Many children and young people see a happy home life as one in which they spend time together as a family, doing things together</li><li>Children and young people dislike arguments between their parents, and of being brought into the conflict by their parents</li><li>Adults and professionals emphasised the importance of encouraging parents to engage with their children, listen to their voices, and allow them to choose their own behaviour within reasonable limits</li><li>Strong close relationships in a family are an invaluable emotional resource in helping children to develop resilience</li><li>There is a need for parenting education to help those who find it difficult, to learn how to be a good parent, but without undermining parental confidence and self-worth</li></ul>	<ul><li>75% of children believe that other people messing about in lessons makes it difficult to learn, and teachers need to address this</li><li>Many children like school because they can be with friends</li><li>Children admire teachers who are passionate about their subjects and who make lessons interesting and fun, and are supportive and kind</li><li>A number of children feel teachers could interact with their pupils better, be more understanding and respectful, and make lessons more challenging</li><li>Many children consider a supportive, respectful and friendly school/classroom environment with a positive approach to tackling bullying important</li><li>Some children would like more time and space to play at school</li><li>55% of children spend more than 1 hour on the internet every day for school work</li><li>22% of children use the internet for more than 2 hours a day</li><li>Many children dislike the pressure that schoolwork and teachers place on them, i.e. tests and exam stress which result in some children self-harming</li><li>49% of children feel under a lot of pressure at school</li><li>58% of 14- to 16-year-olds worry about exams and 47% 14- to 16-year-olds worry about their schoolwork</li><li>40% of children consider that they have a say in the running of their school, e.g. giving an opinion, school council</li><li>44% of children consider that they do not have a say in the running of their school</li><li>Some children feel that teachers rarely listen to or act on their suggestions</li><li>Some children consider that the focus at school is too academic, has limited practical application outside school, with insufficient personal and social development</li><li>The right of children to participate in decisions that affect them was highlighted by a number of adults as being important</li></ul>

Table 3.2 National reports and pupil voice

IPPR Freedom's Orphans. Raising Youth in a Changing World	UNICEF Child Poverty in Perspective
Background	**Background**
The research, published in 2006, was based on two large surveys that followed young people born in 1958 and 1970. The research explored the notion that British youth are on the verge of mental breakdown, at risk of anti-social behaviour, self-harm, drug and alcohol abuse, and that a number of them come from lower socio-economic groups, which strongly determines their futures.	UNICEF Report Card 7, 'Child Poverty in Perspective: An overview of Child Well-being in Rich Countries' was published in February 2007. It compared the well-being of children and young people in 21 of the world's richest countries. The research focused on six different aspects: child poverty; health and safety; education; relationships with family and friends; behaviours and risks; and subjective well-being.
Main findings	**Main findings**
■ British youth have been left to their own devices for too long	■ The best place to be a child or young person is in the Netherlands
■ British teenagers spend more time with friends than with parents/adults	■ The worst place to be a child or young person is in the UK
■ Only 1.2 million of 4.6 million 11–16-year-olds have access to youth clubs	■ The UK ranks in the bottom third of 21 countries for five of the six aspects.
■ 1 in 4 young people have access to structured youth activities	These are relative poverty and deprivation; quality of children's relationships
■ British children spend half their spare time watching TV, playing computer games and using the internet, even before the age of 10	with their parents and peers; child health and safety; behaviour and risk taking; and subjective well-being. The UK ranks higher in the educational dimension.
■ 8 out of 10 children aged 5–16 have a TV in their bedroom, and 1 in 5 (1.5 million) have internet access in their bedroom	■ 20.1% of UK children said they did not have all the things they need to do schoolwork at home
■ 65% of children and young people have their own mobile phone	■ 9.4% of UK children have fewer than 10 books at home
■ 12% of 11–15 year olds have taken cannabis in the last 12 months	■ 14.5% UK children live in step families
■ British adolescents are the third worst binge drinkers in Europe	■ 16.9% of UK young people live in single-parent families
■ Only 30% of adults would challenge young people behaving anti-socially	■ 60.5% of UK children say parents often spend time just talking to them
	■ 66.7% of UK children say they eat with parents more than once a week
Recommendations	■ 43.3% of young people in the UK find other young people kind and helpful
■ Every child and young person should do at least 1 hour per week of constructive after-school activities	(lowest in UNICEF report)
■ Media and marketing should be regulated to reduce child consumerism	■ 35.8% of UK young people had been bullied in the last 2 months
■ Teenage pregnancies should be reduced	■ 43.9% of UK young people had been in a fight in the last year
■ Fair opportunities for young people to participate in extra-curricular activities and youth club activities should be provided	■ 6.8% of UK young people feel like an outsider or left out of things
■ Promotion of positive activities through the voluntary sector should occur	■ 5.4% of UK young people feel lonely
■ Introduce financial asset accounts for looked-after children to support transition and independent living	■ 19.0% of UK young people agreed that they like school a lot
■ Improve initial teacher training by including conflict resolution, meeting diverse needs of pupils, pedagogic techniques	■ 22.6% of UK young people rated their health as fair or poor
■ Bring back school house systems in state schools to break up peer group hierarchies and gangs	The UNICEF report provided a wake-up call to the government.
■ Communities should be supported to socialise young people effectively	

CfBT The voice of young people: an engine for improvement

Background

CfBT commissioned NFER to undertake a literature review of existing research on pupil voice. The research focused on exploring the impact of young people's voice (aged 11–19) on policy making and practice, and what schools, organisations and services are doing as a result of such insights.

Main findings

- There is a growing culture of participation, with insights and ideas from the younger generation recognised as valuable in potentially shaping services and policies which affect their lives and others in the community
- The engagement of young people in these matters can have diverse impacts on the young people involved at personal, school, wider community and societal levels
- There is a relative 'gap' in any routine systematic in-depth evaluation and documentation of the impact of young people's participation, voice and involvement
- The impact of young people's voice on policy and practice resulted in:
  – changes in organisational practices, services and facilities
  – strategy and policy development
  – impact on budgetary decision making
  – the production of materials and information resources
- The positive impact of young people's voice on the young people themselves which includes:
  – increased confidence and self-esteem
  – improved social, personal and emotional competence
  – increased sense of responsibility, efficacy and autonomy
  – acquisition of new knowledge and skills
  – enhanced communication and collaborative skills
  – civic and political competence
  – improved school attendance, achievement and behaviour

Recommendations

- Organisations should ensure that the outcomes of young people's involvement should be properly evaluated and recorded
- Young people themselves should say what they think the impact and advantages of their contributions have been to them personally
- Impacts arising from young people's input should be tracked in longer term

JRF Parenting – children's voice in ordinary families

Background

Joseph Rowntree Foundation (JRF) sought the findings from seven reviews of existing research on parenting in ordinary families to better understand diversity in parenting and its implications for family policies and support services. The topics covered by the seven reviews included: parenting and outcomes for children; parenting and resilience; fathers and fatherhood; parenting and ethnicity; children's views of parenting; parenting and poverty; barriers to inclusion. The final report *Parenting and the different ways it can affect children's lives* was published in August 2007.

Main findings

- What young people think is not necessarily what adults think they think
- Parents often fail to understand what their children go through during emotional disturbances such as bullying, exam time
- The way parents behave, their attitudes and feelings do impact on children's upbringing
- Young people generally dislike feeling overprotected by their parents/adults
- Children dislike family conflict
- Children and young people like to be consulted by parents
- Warm, authoritative and responsive parenting is crucial to building resilience in children and young people
- 1 in 10 children regard their upbringing as 'very strict' with parental discipline being based on reasoning, explanation and non-physical punishments
- Teenagers of either sex feel closer to their mother than to their father
- Parents' engagement in family support services can be improved by more accessible venues and times for service delivery; a better 'visible' mix of staff by age, gender and ethnicity; and trusting relationships between staff and parents

Table 3.2 Continued.

SCUK school councils – school improvement	DCSF real decision making? School councils in action
Background	**Background**
School Councils UK commissioned in-depth action research between September 2004 and July 2007 in eight London secondary schools, to explore the potential of genuine pupil participation to improve schools. The research focused on pupils' involvement in the aspects of behaviour; health and well-being; school management; and teaching and learning. The final report was published in September 2007.	The purpose of the research was to inform future government guidance for schools on involving pupils in decision making, including the work of school councils. The research undertaken during 2006–2007 included a review of the current literature, national surveys and school case studies. The research aimed to understand the role of school councils in supporting pupil voice; explore the range of current practice and identify examples of good practice.
Main Findings	**Main findings**
■ 66% of schools saw an improvement in relationships between pupils	■ Up to 95% of schools in England and Wales have a school council
■ 58% of schools reported an improvement in relationships between staff and pupils	■ 62% of teachers felt school councils should be compulsory in England
■ 65% of teachers in the schools involved in lesson observations thought that the school council made a positive impact on teaching and learning	■ Most school councils tackle issues relating to the school environment and facilities, rather than teaching and learning
■ 70% of schools saw a positive impact on pupils' self-esteem	■ school councils vary in England in relation to how they operate
■ 71% of teachers saw an improvement in pupils' decision making	■ 1 in 10 school councils are merely 'talking shops'
Recommendations	■ Successful school councils rely on the school having a clear rationale for introducing pupil voice provision, and on providing training for pupils
■ School councils could usefully be made compulsory in schools, but only if they are timetabled and funded	■ Just under 45% of teachers would like like pupils involved in the process of appointing teachers
■ School council work should be accredited	■ 33% of teachers would like to see pupil representation on governing bodies
■ School councils should have a central role and not merely be consultative, in helping to formulate and create policy	■ Schools would benefit from greater support in designing pupil voice provision for the full diversity of pupils, e.g. those with SEN/LDD
■ School council work needs monitoring	■ Ensuring pupils have a good understanding of their rights and responsibilities helps to prevent any inappropriate expressions of pupil voice occurring
■ School council pupils need to be accepted as professionals because of their considerable experience and expertise on teaching and learning, behaviour and school climate	**Recommendations**
■ School councils need the direct oversight and validation of the head teacher	■ School councils should be regarded as being one component of pupil voice
■ There need to be clear lines of communication from the school council through class councils, year councils, and executive groups so that an individual voice can be heard and quick feedback given	■ There should be improved pupil–governing body communication
	■ The government should produce updated guidance on pupil participation
	■ Good practice in school councils should be more widely disseminated
	■ School leaders should develop a pupil voice policy to guide their work
	■ Pupils should be involved in the production of the School Development Plan
	■ School councils should be given a budget for activities (0.05% of overall school budget)

The Primary Review – Community Soundings

Background

The Primary Review was launched in October 2006 by the University of Cambridge. Its purpose was to examine how well the current system of primary education is doing, how it could be improved and how primary schools should respond to national and global challenges. The review focused on ten broad themes which were covered in 32 interim reports. These themes were: purpose and values; learning and teaching; curriculum and assessment; quality and standards; diversity and inclusion; settings and professionals; parenting, caring and education; beyond the school; structures and phases; funding and governance. Children were one of the main stakeholder groups giving their views. The first interim report *Community Soundings* was published in October 2007. The main overall Primary Review report will be published in late 2008.

Main findings – Community Soundings

- Today's children are under intense and excessive pressure from the policy driven demands of their schools and the commercially driven values of the wider society
- Family life and community are breaking down
- Respect and empathy are in decline both within and between generations
- Life beyond the school gates is increasingly insecure and dangerous
- The primary curriculum is too rigidly prescribed and, due to the pressure of national tests, too narrow
- Primary pupils' educational careers are being distorted by the dominance of the national tests, especially in Years 5 and 6
- Some government initiatives in the areas of curriculum, assessment and pedagogy are constraining and disempowering rather than enabling learners
- The Every Child Matters ideal of equipping learners with broader life skills, while warmly welcomed, appears to be at odds with the current emphasis on target setting, testing and academic achievement in a narrow range of subjects

---

Children as victims: child-sized crimes in a child-sized world

Background

The Howard League for Penal Reform, as part of the Citizenship and Crime project that ran in primary and secondary schools between 1997 and 2006, surveyed more than 3,000 children across the country, publishing their final report in October 2007.

Main findings

- 95% of children surveyed had been a victim of crime on at least one occasion
- 49% of children had had property stolen from them at school
- 57% had had personal property deliberately damaged
- Nearly three-quarters of children in the survey had been assaulted
- 56% had been threatened on at least one occasion
- 46% had been called racist names
- Children predominantly reported their victimisation to family members and friends
- Only a third reported incidents to the police or teachers
- The majority of victimisation incidents were low level and took place in schools and playgrounds
- Children's ideas for preventing crime were to have more local activities for children and young people; provide more child-friendly cafes, skate parks and youth clubs
- Children want more safe places provided for them, more active listening, and confidence that something will be done about their problems
- Children are rarely consulted about the impact of crime on their lives
- Some children don't bother to report crimes because they think adults will not listen to them, or the crime is too minor to be considered
- Children are concerned that adults don't fully understand how to respond to such incidents and thus take little action
- Conflict resolution, mediation and restorative justice introduced into schools help to prevent crime and victimisation

Recommendations

- Children need to be listened to and included in all future proposals and policies affecting their lives
- Utilising a bottom-up local partnership approach based in schools helps to educate children about crime and victimisation
- Listen to children talk about their own experiences as victims, helping them to develop social skills, self-esteem and assertiveness

Table 3.2 Continued.

Primary Review – **Children and their Primary Schools: pupils' voices**	Primary Review – **Children's Lives Outside School and their Educational Impact**
Background This interim report as part of the Primary Review was published in November 2007. **Main findings** ■ Children's voices matter ■ There is a need to build on children's active role in their learning ■ There is a need to respect their rights and build upon children's views ■ Enhanced pupil voice challenges the traditional teacher–pupil power relationship in the classroom ■ More equal power relations between teachers, the head teacher and pupils leads to more equal and negotiated decision making ■ The key aim of pupil voice work is to challenge traditional teacher–pupil power relationships which curtail and inhibit the embedding of equality of voice for all ■ The recent inclusion of Citizenship Education within the primary curriculum is helping to develop a sense of responsibility in pupils, and to make pupils more aware of their rights and responsibilities as learners and citizens beyond the classroom and school ■ Overall findings suggest that the voices and views of pupils are not always heard in their schools, and that many schools have some way to go in taking pupils' perspectives into consideration ■ There needs to be a move towards including pupils as active participants in the school where their voices are listened to ■ Pupils should no longer be moulded to fit into existing systems and structures but should be members of a school which is built around listening to and providing for their needs ■ Pupil voice is not a vehicle for trying to discipline, control, erode or reform teachers' professionalism ■ Pupil voice should be an aspect covered in Initial Teacher Training (ITT) and ongoing continuing professional development (CPD) for qualified teachers, from the perspective of how pupil voice can be successfully embedded in daily teaching and learning classroom practice. This will help to allay teacher apprehension and anxieties about pupil voice ■ There should be a teacher responsible for coordinating and leading pupil voice activities in the school ■ Every Child Matters is providing enhanced opportunities to consult with and listen to pupils' voice and views	**Background** This interim report as part of the Primary Review was published in November 2007. **Main findings** ■ Children value their free time. Home allows for this but school doesn't ■ Children's lives in England have become increasingly scholarised and under adult surveillance in recent years ■ As children's lives become increasingly scholarised they may wish to defend their home as their 'private space', separate from an educational environment ■ Children's independent mobility in public spaces has diminished, due to 'stranger danger' and adults' obsession with risk assessments ■ Children's lives are becoming dominated by technology at home and at school, e.g. engagement with computers, the internet, TV and DVD, mobile phones ■ Parents need to give careful consideration to how far they create an educational environment in the home for their children, without compromising their child's work–life balance ■ Children indicated that they wish for, but generally fail to get respect for themselves as persons at school. They want to be treated in a more adult way ■ Those responsible for primary education have a duty to respect children's rights at school on the basis of the United Nations Convention on the Rights of the Child (UNCRC) ■ Schools have a duty (within the terms of the UNCRC) to work towards democratising their ethos and practices

DCSF Time to Talk Consultation	PIRLS Readers and Reading National Report for England 2006
Background 'Time to Talk' national community consultation took place during September and October 2007. It sought the views of children and young people as one of a range of stakeholders, about issues facing children and young people's well-being. These views informed the government's Children Plan, launched in December 2007. 'Time to Talk' focused on key themes: family and others; staying safe; enjoying and achieving; being good/making a positive contribution. **Main findings** ■ 41% of children and young people are concerned about their personal safety at school and in the community ■ 21% of children and young people are concerned about bullying ■ 21% of children and young people are worried about their education ■ 11% of children and young people are most concerned about tests and exams ■ 12% of young people consider the community needs to understand them better ■ 20% of young people want more youth clubs and activities in the community ■ 30% of young people consider the community does nothing to support them ■ 66% of children and young people consider providing more activities is the key to keeping them out of trouble after school and at the weekends ■ 18% of children said that parents should encourage them ■ 13% of children said that parents should listen to them ■ 53% of young people said that services should ask their opinions and listen to them ■ Children and young people want to be listened to, respected, treated as equals and have their views taken into account by parents ■ Young people want to feel listened to, included and consulted by the adults they come into contact with ■ Children and young people want more school counsellors, to help them when they have problems ■ Children and young people felt that too often their viewpoint was disregarded which made them feel rebellious ■ Children and young people believe in mutual respect, and consider that feeling supported by friends, family and teachers is important in building their confidence ■ Children and young people call for more opportunities at school to help their communities and charities	**Background** This report is the second rigorous international survey which compares the reading attainment, reading habits and attitudes to reading of over 200,000 9–10-year-old children in 41 countries. The report was published in November 2007. **Main findings** ■ English children have the least positive attitudes to reading ■ They are reading fewer novels and stories outside school on a daily basis than they were in 2001, and compared to their peers in other countries ■ Children's busy days leave less time for books at home which compete with TV and computer games ■ 37% of England's 10-year-olds play computer/video games for more than 3 hours a day, which is more than their peers in other countries ■ The highest achieving children are reading less in their free time ■ Only a third of children in England reported reading for fun on a daily basis ■ Reading needs to be part of children's routines with families reading together ■ 8% of children have no books at home in England ■ A child from a deprived home has heard just 13 million words by the age of four, compared to 45 million words of a child from a more affluent home ■ Girls are more likely than boys to undertake reading activities inside and outside school ■ Only 37% of 10-year-olds in England feel safe in the classroom ■ English children were ranked 37 out of 45 in an international league table comparing children's fear of theft, bullying and assault ■ 70% of children in England liked being in school, but this was one of the smallest proportions worldwide ■ 59% of pupils in England said that someone in their class had been injured by another pupil ■ 30% of England's 10-year-olds said they had been bullied in the last month ■ 52% of pupils in England said that bullying had affected someone in their class ■ 78% of pupils in England agreed that children in their school helped each other with their work, which is broadly in line with the international average ■ 74% of pupils in England believed that children in their school cared about each other, which is broadly in line with the international average ■ 85% of pupils in England thought that teachers in their school cared about them, which is around the international average

The intention and aim in this chapter is to highlight the main findings and recommendations from the most recent leading surveys and reports undertaken in 2007, and to provide guidance as to how this information can help schools and other educational settings to strengthen their own practice in pupil voice and participation in decision making, in order to improve the Every Child Matters well-being outcomes.

Further activities are provided at the end of the chapter, which should enable solution-focused exploration and new developments to occur at whole school, or classroom level.

Guidance on using the information from national surveys and reports

1 Read the overview summaries of the main findings and recommendations arising from the national context.
2 Identify common themes, strands and similarities existing in the current national surveys and reports that children and young people have raised.
3 Negotiate with key stakeholders, including the pupils themselves, a whole school survey which is informed by the national concerns, to cross-check with the national perspective of children and young people.
4 Following analysis of the findings from the school survey, draw up an action plan with no more than three priorities that pupils have identified.
5 Feedback to pupils and other stakeholders why the three priorities have been selected, and make clear what the expectations are in addressing these.
6 Ensure the priorities fit in with the School Development Plan priorities for Every Child Matters and personalised learning.
7 Ensure the findings from the school survey and the resulting action feed into the school's SEF, and clearly indicate the impact pupil voice has had in improving Every Child Matters well-being outcomes.

Guidance on engaging pupil voice 'face-to-face'

Use the following checklist to guide you through the process of engaging and encouraging pupil voice at an individual or class group level, as part of personalised learning.

- Put pupils at their ease before commencing discussion by using 'icebreaker' activities
- Refer pupils to the school/class code of conduct on pupil voice to remind them of procedures and their rights
- Emphasise confidentiality and reassure pupils that their responses will be anonymous, prior to commencing discussion with pupils
- Explain clearly to pupils the reason for seeking their views
- Avoid putting words into children's mouths by not asking leading questions
- Ask pupils clear questions that don't mislead, and preferably questions that pupils have generated themselves on an issue of concern to them
- Ensure the environment, climate and ethos where pupils are sharing their views and ideas is emotionally intelligent, and not intimidating
- Actively listen to what pupils have to say, giving them the time to elaborate on their views and opinions
- Remain impartial to pupils' views, especially when they may be contrary to your own, or those of other pupils
- Ask pupils to justify and give a reason for the views and opinions they have expressed

- Check your understanding of pupils' responses back with them to clarify meaning, e.g. 'So, when you say . . . you really mean . . .'
- Ensure pupils understand the extent to which their views can realistically be acted upon
- Inform pupils about how their ideas will be taken into account and taken forward
- Ensure all pupils have equality of opportunity to contribute their views and ideas, and don't let the most vocal pupils monopolise the discussion
- Offer a range of alternative ways to direct discussion for those pupils who find oral communication problematic, e.g. visual representation – mind maps, symbols and picture cards, voting buttons
- Explain to pupils, through follow-up feedback discussions, why their views have not on this occasion influenced change, and give pupils the opportunity to ask further questions.

Further activities

The following questions, based on those that children and young people were asked in key national surveys and reports, are designed to enable you to discuss and identify the current and future position within your own educational setting with pupils, staff and other stakeholders collectively. Use the following questions to help you to clarify what pupils really think about school and local issues, thereby enabling improvements in children and young people's well-being to begin to be addressed.

Questions for pupils

- How often are you able to give your views, ideas and opinions on important school issues?
- What is it about this school/class that helps you to have a say?
- Who inspires you to express your views and ideas in school?
- Who inspires you to express your views and ideas outside school?
- How far do you feel that what pupils say makes a difference in your school?
- Who could help pupils in school/class to make things better for children?
- What worries you most in school?
- What worries you most outside school and in the local community?
- What would make your own and the lives of others better in this school/class?
- What could you and other pupils do to make things better in this school or class?
- What factors do you think make for a good, happy childhood?
- What stops pupils in this school/class/local community from having good well-being, and a happy, healthy childhood?
- What changes could be made to improve pupil well-being and happiness in this school/class?
- What do you think are the most important things that make for a good life for pupils in this school/class/local community?
- How can the school/class teachers ensure that pupils feel treated fairly and with respect?
- How can the school reduce any pupil bullying and make children feel safer in school?
- What support would pupils welcome to stop other pupils from getting them into trouble?

Questions for senior leaders/classroom practitioners

- What pupil consultation processes are already in place at whole school and classroom level, to review school policy and practice?
- What process exists in school for pupils to resolve any unfair behaviour from adults?
- How could school leaders build in more quality time for staff and pupils to undertake more pupil voice activities?

- To what extent does your school/classroom culture and ethos promote the further development of pupil voice and participation?
- How can less assertive and reticent pupils be supported and encouraged to participate, and have more of a say?
- What am I aiming to achieve and what do I expect in relation to pupil voice?
- What will the pupils in the school/my class get out of pupil voice activities and participation?
- How can I ensure that pupil voice becomes part of every day practice?

4

Every Child Matters Pupil Voice Toolkit

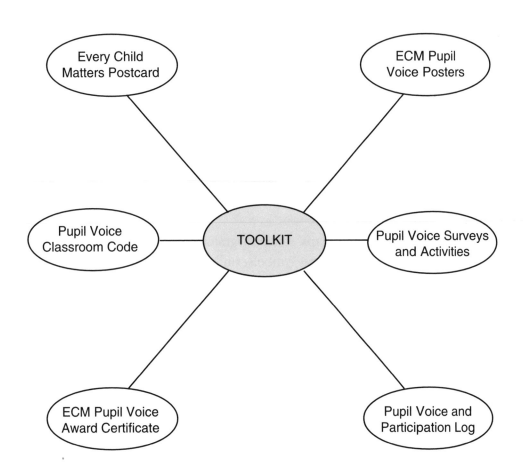

This chapter comprises a range of practical resources which can be adapted and customised to suit the context of the educational setting. The model materials provided in the chapter are generic, and therefore are appropriate for pupils in the primary and secondary phase of education. The majority of the resources in the toolkit are for use at classroom level with pupils. Some of the resources seek pupils' views directly. Other materials promote and acknowledge pupil voice and participation achievements.

The materials in this chapter are suggested ideas that class teachers, in particular, may find useful as a starting-point and stimulus for engaging pupil voice.

Model surveys for governors and for parents and carers have been included near the end of the chapter. They ensure that these important stakeholders have an opportunity to share their views about pupil voice and Every Child Matters (ECM). The ECM quiz is provided as a familiarisation activity to use with adults and older pupils and students in the secondary and FE sector. The toolkit acts as a launch pad for further pupil voice activities related to Every Child Matters. It is envisaged that those using the materials will wish to add their own resources to the toolkit. Other external frontline practitioners working directly with children in school will also have useful tools to add, which engage pupil voice.

Methods of seeking and engaging pupil voice

The methods listed below for seeking and engaging pupil voice provide a useful point of reference and can be added to.

- Individual pupil interviews and focused discussions
- Focused group discussions and interviews
- Grouping and ranking exercises
- Pupil voice communication passports
- Visual representations, e.g. mind maps, spider diagrams, flow charts, mosaic approach – montage of visual images/photographs, symbols, smiley faces, PECS, Makaton
- Problem pages
- Video clips and diary room
- Suggestion boxes
- Questionnaires and surveys
- Pupil summits and conferences
- Focus groups, forums, working groups, action groups, panels
- Pupil local networks and cluster groups
- Electronic communication – email, text messaging, 'blogging', chat rooms, electronic discussion forums, voting buttons
- Circle time
- Formal forums – school council, pupil associate governors, Youth Parliament
- Pupils as researchers, inspectors/evaluators
- Assemblies – whole school or class, 'Jerry Springer'-type debates
- Pupil attendance in school formal management processes – curriculum, staff, governors, senior leadership team meetings and INSET

Four popular approaches used in schools for consulting with pupils and seeking their views are as follows:

1 **an occasional referendum** – i.e. pupils' opinions in a particular year group, or whole school, are gathered via class representations on the school council, pupil discussion forums or questionnaire

2   **a regular forum** – i.e. circle time, class discussions, electronic forums
3   **one-to-one interviews or small-group focused discussions** – with a particular subgroup of pupils about how they feel about the ECM outcomes in school, and what could be done to improve their achievements in relation to their well-being
4   **an enquiry** – on ECM designed by teacher and/or pupils, which involves pupils as researchers who collect the views of their peers, analyse their research findings, and summarise the outcomes for peers and staff.

Have your say postcard

Every Child Matters in Leafy Lane School

What I like best about
Every Child Matters
in school is?

What more should be done in school
to make the Every Child Matters
outcomes better for pupils?

Figure 4.1

This Log belongs to

_____

During this term I have:

Shared an idea with the class.   YES ☐   NO ☐

My idea was: _____

Expressed a view about a school issue.   YES ☐ NO ☐

The view I expressed was: _____

My view has helped to bring about a change. YES ☐ NO ☐

I have made a decision this term.   YES ☐   NO ☐

Pupil Voice and Participation Log

Leafy Lane School

My target for **next** term for pupil voice and participation is:

_____
_____

The support I need to meet this target will be:

_____
_____

Those who can help me to meet this target in school are:

_____
_____

Signature: _____

Date: _____

The decision I made was: _____
_____

I would like to become more involved in making changes and improvements in school.

YES ☐   NO ☐

The ways in which I would like to be involved are:

_____
_____

My target for having a say and making a positive contribution for **this** term was:

_____
_____

I have met ☐   not met this target ☐

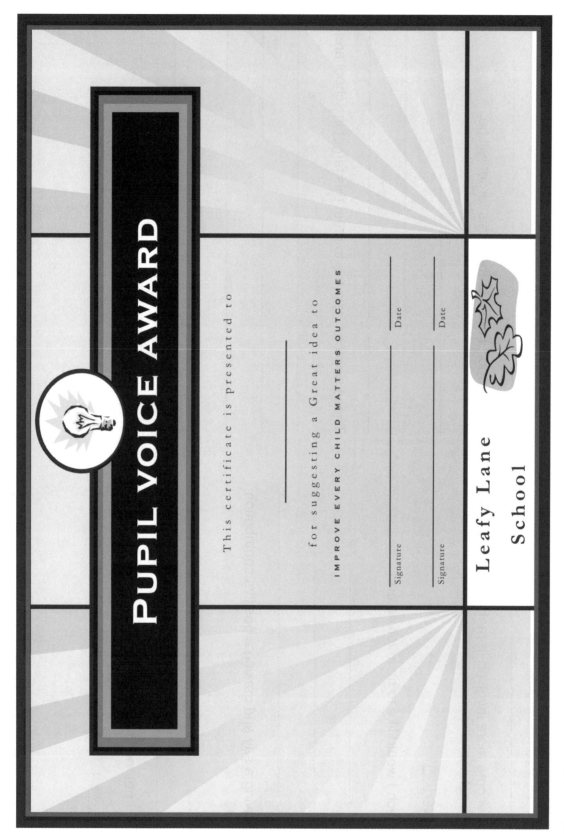

Figure 4.3

My pupil voice passport

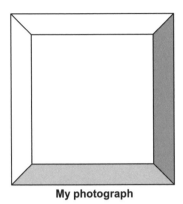

My photograph

Name:

Form:

The best way(s) I can influence change and decision-making in school is by:

The issue that concerns me the most in relation to children and young people's safety in the local community is:

The community activities I have been involved in this term have been:

The one new pupil voice activity I really want to be involved in next year is:

Put a circle around what you are good at:

Team work	Making decisions	Problem solving
Being a responsible citizen	Listening to others	Volunteering and helping others
Getting my point of view across		

Other life skills I am good at:

The things I really care about in school are:

The things that concern me most about learning, well-being and school life in general are:

The one thing I want to change most in school is:

The one thing I value the most about having a say in how the school is run is:

Put a circle around the pupil voice activities you have participated in this year.

Circle time	In-class discussion	Focus Group
School Council Member	Pupil mentor/ Pupil counsellor	
Survey/ Questionnaire	Voting buttons	Suggestion box
Pupil researcher	Pupil summit	
Video diary room		

Other pupil voice activities:

In my leisure time outside school, the things I enjoy doing that make a positive contribution are:

Figure 4.4

This activity can be undertaken by staff and pupils separately, and then cross-checked to identify common priorities for future action.

At the moment pupils at this school in relation to Every Child Matters . . .	
Think?	**Feel?**
Say?	**Do?**

In three years' time, we want pupils at this school to . . .	
Think?	**Feel?**
Say?	**Do?**

Source: Adapted from DCSF 2007e: 31

Figure 4.5 Pupil voice and involvement in ECM decision making

Pupil voice tracker

How to use the pupil voice tracker

- During each day of the week, think about the ways you have given your views and ideas

- At the end of each day write in examples of pupil voice activities

- Look at the box on the right of this page to remind you what pupil voice means

Pupil voice means

- To have a say in how the school is run

- To give your views and opinions

- To share your ideas and views with others

- To take part in the school's decision making

- To take part in what happens in school

- To take an interest in what goes on in school

Name: **Class:**

Day of the week	Lessons/subjects which have pupil voice activities	Pupil voice activities and outcomes for you/other pupils
MONDAY		
TUESDAY		
WEDNESDAY		
THURSDAY		
FRIDAY		

Week beginning:

Figure 4.6

Pupil voice survey (primary phase)

Answer the questions below by ticking the relevant boxes

1. My school likes me to talk about things that are important to pupils.
   YES ☐   NO ☐

2. I am asked what I think about any changes the school wants to make.
   YES ☐   NO ☐

3. Adults in school listen to me, when I am asked to give my views or an idea.
   YES ☐   NO ☐

4. I am always told why my ideas cannot be used.
   YES ☐   NO ☐

5. I get a reward, certificate or class points when my views or ideas are used.
   YES ☐   NO ☐

6. I think my views and ideas are taken seriously in this school.
   YES ☐   NO ☐

7. I feel I have a real say in how the school is run.
   YES ☐   NO ☐

8. If I have a different view to that of others I am put down by adults in school.
   YES ☐   NO ☐

9. The one best way I like to get my views and ideas across to adults is
   (Tick **ONE** box only)

   online   voting slips &   survey or   post-it
   consultation ☐   buttons ☐   questionnaire ☐   notes ☐

   use   mind   tell
   pictures ☐   map ☐   someone ☐

   other ways (please state): _____

   _____

10. If I could ask the head teacher one thing to help give pupils more of a
    say in matters that affect them, I would ask the head to .....?

   _____

   _____

   _____

Thank you for completing this survey.
Please post it in the box in the main school entrance.

Figure 4.7

Pupil voice survey – making a positive contribution

Please take time to answer the following questions. Your responses will be confidential and anonymous.

Male ☐   Female ☐   Form/Class ☐

Questions

1. How does the school seek the views of pupils on learning, well-being and school life in general?

2. How much do you feel the views of pupils are listened to and acted upon in relation to Every Child Matters outcomes?

3. How are pupils being kept informed of the progress being made in acting on their views to improve Every Child Matters in school?

4. Place a tick ✓ in the relevant boxes to show the pupil voice activities you have been involved in this year.

Voted in school, class or year elections ☐	Taken part in a pupil summit ☐	Made a presentation to staff ☐
Made a presentation to governors ☐	Member of a working party ☐	School council member ☐
Member of Pupil Parliament ☐	Pupil researcher ☐	Class/Form representative ☐
Helping appoint staff in school ☐	Helping to organise a Pupil Conference ☐	

Any other pupil voice activity (please state what this is): _____

_____

5. How well-informed do you feel about what the school is doing to improve the Every Child Matters outcomes for pupils?

Well-informed ☐   Not well-informed ☐

6. How have your parents/carers supported you in having a greater 'voice' and choice about Every Child Matters in school?

7. In the last year what have you done to make a positive contribution in school?

8. What have you done in the last year to make a positive contribution in the local community?

9. What else could you do in school, or in the local community, to increase your participation?

10. Is there anything else you wish to tell us about pupil involvement, participation or consultation in school?

Thank you for taking the time to complete this survey.
Please post your completed survey in the post box in the school's reception area.

Figure 4.8

Pupils and parents/carers Every Child Matters survey

Leafy Lane School values the views of pupils and their parents/carers on how well we are doing in meeting the five Every Child Matters outcomes which are:

- Be healthy

- Stay safe

- Enjoy and achieve

- Make a positive contribution

- Achieve economic well-being

Please answer all the questions below and return this survey to the school reception ECM post box.

Place a ✓ in the relevant boxes

I am a parent/carer ☐   I am a pupil ☐

Questions

1. Does the school make the five Every Child Matters outcomes very clear to pupils, parents/carers?
   YES ☐   NO ☐

   If no, what else could the school do to make the Every Child Matters clearer?

2. Do you feel you have been given the opportunity throughout the school year to give your views and opinions on Every Child Matters?
   YES ☐   NO ☐

   If no, please state how you would wish to have more of a say about Every Child Matters at Leafy Lane School.

3. Which Every Child Matters outcomes does Leafy Lane School do well in and why?

4. Which, if any, Every Child Matters outcome(s) needs improving at Leafy Lane School?

5. How could this/these Every Child Matters outcome(s) be improved in Leafy Lane School?

6. What would you like to see happen next at Leafy Lane School that would make Every Child Matters outcomes even better for its pupils?

7. What do you think matters most to pupils in Leafy Lane School?

8. Is there any further comment you wish to make about Every Child Matters in the school? If so, please write your comment below.

Thank you for taking the time to complete this annual school survey.
Please return your completed survey to the post box in the school's main reception area.

Figure 4.9

School governors' pupil voice survey

1. How often do you hear about Every Child Matters achievements in school, directly from the pupils?

2. How do you get to know the pupils' views about Every Child Matters in school?

3. How will you gain a clear view about the school's strengths in the Every Child Matters outcomes?

4. What are the school's weaknesses and areas for further development in Every Child Matters?

5. In your role as a school governor what could you do to enable pupils to have a greater 'voice' about Every Child Matters?

6. What really matters to pupils in Leafy Lane School in relation to the Every Child Matters outcomes?

7. What has been the value added in relation to improving pupils' Every Child Matters well-being outcomes?

8. In which Every Child Matters outcome(s) does the school achieve best in?

9. Where are the gaps in Every Child Matters provision in school?

10. How are pupils currently involved in governing body meetings at school in order to enable them to make a positive contribution?

11. Is pupil involvement and 'voice' enough in the school and on the governing body? If not, how could it be improved?

Figure 4.10

Examples of pupil voice and participation activities

These pupil-led activities can be used at a class or whole school level.
They are appropriate for primary and secondary schools.

Activity 1
The pupils in your class want to know more about Articles 12 and 13 of the United Nations Convention on the Rights of the Child.
You and three other pupils have been asked to present Articles 12 and 13 in a more pupil-friendly way, to the whole class.
You need to involve as many pupils as possible in this activity.

Activity 2
The school council has decided to hold a competition to see which class can produce the best 'Every Child Matters Rights Treaty' for school.
The winning entry will be displayed in all classrooms and around the school.
he class has one month to work on producing a treaty.

Activity 3
A recent school survey showed that exam stress was the biggest worry for pupils.
The head teacher has asked to meet with the Pupil Well-Being Focus Group next week, to discuss the issue and find a solution to the problem.
The pupils collectively in the class need to suggest ideas for reducing pupils' examination stress in school.
These ideas will be submitted for the meeting next week.

Activity 4
The local police are launching a campaign STAY SAFE – EVERY CHILD MATTERS IN THIS COMMUNITY, in response to the recent negative reports about some children and young people's anti-social behaviour in the town centre at night.
A group of pupils from your school have been invited to attend the local roadshow about the campaign.
Suggest ideas for how children and young people can enjoy leisure activities and play together safely, out of school hours in the local community.
Ideas must be realistic, as pupils from the school will be involved in putting some of the best ideas into practice.

Figure 4.11

Model pupil voice classroom code

All pupils in this classroom:

- **Listen when others are speaking**

- **Do not talk at the same time when others are speaking**

- **Respect and value the views, ideas and feelings of others**

- **Never put others down for having a different view or opinion**

- **Operate a 'no blame' culture by never naming and shaming others**

- **Take on and share responsibilities willingly**

- **Make sensible decisions, choices and positive contributions**

- **Are open and honest**

- **Apologise for any unpleasant or unhelpful comments expressed**

- **Enjoy taking part in discussions**

Figure 4.12

Every Child Matters in Leafy Lane School and in this classroom.

What have you achieved today to improve your learning and well-being?

Figure 4.13

Everyone's views and ideas are valued and respected in Leafy Lane School.

Don't be afraid to speak out and have your say.

Figure 4.14

Every Child Matters quiz

1. In what year was Every Child Matters first proposed and introduced by the government? (1 mark)

2. How many Every Child Matters outcomes are there? (1 mark)

3. List what the Every Child Matters outcomes are. (5 marks)

4. Who is the Children's Commissioner in England? (1 mark)

5. Which government Minister has overall responsibility for children and young people? (1 mark)

6. What do the following abbreviations mean? (5 marks)

    CAF
    CYPP
    ECM
    NSF
    NHSS

7. What is the website address where you can find out about Every Child Matters? (1 mark)

8. Which three services work together to improve Every Child Matters outcomes for children and young people? (3 marks)

9. In which section of the OFSTED school self-evaluation form (SEF) is Every Child Matters mainly evaluated? (1 mark)

10. The Every Child Matters Green Paper stated that
    'Pupil . . . . and well-being go hand-in-hand'
    What is the missing word that goes after 'Pupil' and before 'and well-being'? (1 mark)

    Total 20 marks

Figure 4.15

ECM Quiz Answers

1. 2003; 2. 5 outcomes; 3. be healthy, stay safe, enjoy and achieve, make a positive contribution, achieve economic well-being; 4. Sir Albert Aynsley-Green; 5. Beverley Hughes; 6. Common Assessment Framework, Children and Young People's Plan, Every Child Matters, National Service Framework, National Healthy School Standard; 7. www.everychildmatters.gov.uk; 8. Education, Health and Social Services; 9. SEF Section 4, Personal Development and Well-being; 10. performance

5

Making a Positive Contribution through Pupil Voice

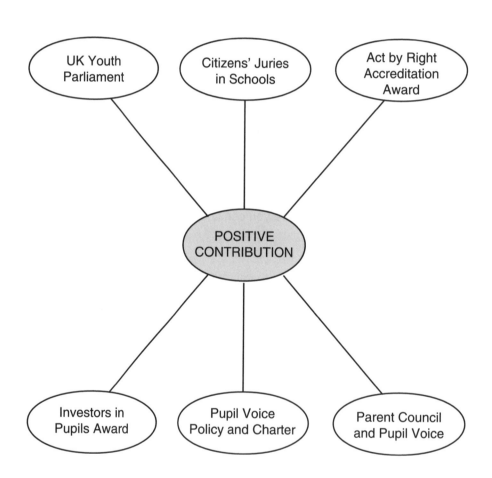

UK Youth Parliament

Citizens' Juries in Schools

Act by Right Accreditation Award

POSITIVE CONTRIBUTION

Investors in Pupils Award

Pupil Voice Policy and Charter

Parent Council and Pupil Voice

The Every Child Matters well-being outcome 'make a positive contribution' aims to ensure that children and young people:

- engage in decision making and support the community and environment
- engage in law-abiding and positive behaviour in and out of school
- develop positive relationships and choose not to bully or discriminate
- develop self-confidence and successfully deal with significant life changes and challenges
- develop enterprising behaviour.

This ECM outcome focuses on the development of the whole child and young person, enabling them to transfer the valuable life skills acquired in school to their lives at home and in the community. Making a positive contribution, as an example of pupil voice, is at the heart of citizenship. Active participation in democracy, understanding rights and responsibilities, and having more of a voice and choice, is crucial to achieving the ECM outcome making a positive contribution, where citizenship is the prime location for ECM issues. PSHE also offers pupils an opportunity to reflect on their personal values, beliefs and their place in the world.

School Councils UK provides an excellent document entitled *School Councils UK Briefing. School Councils and Every Child Matters* (2006), which provides good examples of pupil voice and participation activities aligned with each of the five Every Child Matters outcomes. This can be downloaded free from the website: www.schoolcouncils.org/resources/free-downloads#ECM.

This chapter takes the wider view, looking at pupil voice activities at a more strategic level to inform policy and practice. It provides a useful overview of the UK Youth Parliament, citizens' juries in schools, external awards and accreditation for pupil voice activities, as well as how to engage parents and carers in developing pupil voice.

A model pupil voice policy and a pupil voice charter are included near the end of the chapter. Senior leaders will wish to ensure that pupils are engaged in the process of developing a policy and charter of their own. The chapter closes with a selection of further activities designed to strengthen pupil voice beyond the school.

The UK Youth Parliament

The UK Youth Parliament (UKYP) was launched in July 1999 and it has been operating for nine years. It was originally sponsored by the NSPCC. The UKYP held its first sitting in February 2001 in London. It is an independent national charity and is a non-party political organisation which represents no party political view. It ensures young people aged between 11 and 18 in the UK are given a voice in accordance with Article 12 of the United Nations Convention on the Rights of the Child. It gives some young people the opportunity to be involved in a democratic process at a national level. It empowers young people to take positive action within their local communities based upon issues of shared concern.

Each local authority represents a UKYP constituency. Currently, 90 per cent of the authorities across England are represented on the UKYP, which means that there are over five hundred elected Members of Youth Parliament (MYP) and Deputy Members of Youth Parliament (DMYP), representing young people from a variety of backgrounds, and with a diversity of needs. To become an MYP the young person has to be elected by other young people in an official UKYP election. Elections generally take place between December and February each year.

Once elected, MYPs work to identify the issues of concern locally, regionally or nationally, and then address them through targeted campaigns. Recent campaigns, for example, have led to the establishment of a Youth Board to monitor the media's portrayal of young people, and to work with the Metropolitan Police Service to alter their Standard Operating Procedure on 'stop and search' to ensure young people are treated with respect on the streets.

The UKYP, run by young people for young people, provides a formal opportunity for 11–18-year-olds through 'voice' to bring about social change, and make the world a better place. They represent the views of the young people in their constituency. From 2006 to 2008, 550,000 young people have voted in UKYP elections.

MYPs meet with MPs and local councillors, organise events, run campaigns, make speeches, hold debates, and ensure the views of young people are listened to by decision makers. MYPs have the opportunity to attend between six and ten regional meetings a year during their term of office, which lasts a year. Once every year the UKYP holds an Annual Sitting, which entails a four-day residential, where young people can receive training, plan campaigns, update the UKYP Manifesto, socialise and network. An MYP needs to be able to commit at least five hours every week to UKYP activities.

Other young people who are not MYPs or DMYPs can support UKYP campaigns, debate in UKYP online forums, and participate in consultations. There is a UKYP newsletter which keeps young people informed of developments and activities and a website: www.youthparliament.org.uk.

'Act By Right' Accreditation Award

The UKYP has been working with the National Youth Agency (NYA) who have written the accreditation award Act By Right, to enable young people who have been MYPs and DMYPs to gain this award.

Act By Right comprises five units that support young people through a process of accepting change and evaluating the change. The five units comprise:

1   Getting to know each other and representing others
2   Getting to know the community
3   Getting Ready for Action
4   Campaigning for Change
5   Finding out what's changed.

Each stage requires young people to collect evidence of their work which forms a portfolio of evidence to demonstrate how they have met the aims of each unit. Young people evaluate their efforts against the United Nations Convention on the Rights of the Child.

Each of the five units has three aims, with each aim having three related activities. Act By Right is a 60-hour accreditation award. MYPs and DMYPs are advised to spend ten hours on each unit, with a further ten hours to bring all the work together to complete the journey logs for each unit. Evidence can be in visual, audio and written formats.

A certificate is awarded to those young people fully meeting the requirements. The Award Scheme Development and Accreditation Network (ASDAN) accredit the Act By Right Award. Act By Right is worth one ASDAN point.

Investors in Pupils Award

The award recognises the achievements of the whole school, class groups and individual pupils in five key areas: learning, behaviour, attendance, classroom management and induction. It provides children with opportunities to take responsibility for their own education and behaviour. Work towards achieving the award can be done as part of PSHE. Investors in Pupils (IIP) has a set of four guiding principles, each with a series of indicators and evidence descriptors.

Investors in Pupils enables children to discuss, debate and formulate mission statements, class rules, class targets, individual targets, and a class handbook. It helps pupils to be more aware of the role of staff supporting their learning and well-being in school.

The Investors in Pupils Award was originally created by Catherine Paul, head teacher of Royal Park Primary School in Leeds. It was piloted in primary, secondary and special schools. The Training and Enterprise Council (TEC) revised the award scheme in 2000. In 2001, the Learning and Skills Council (LSC) in West Yorkshire took over responsibility for the award, and funded its delivery until 2006, when the LSC asked the five West Yorkshire education authorities (Bradford, Calderdale, Kirklees, Leeds and Wakefield) to take over the delivery of the award on their behalf. The IIP Partnership plans to roll out Investors in Pupils across the country, working closely with other local authorities.

Investors in Pupils (IIP) is an award that rewards good practice in involving pupils in their own education. IIP builds on the principles of Investors in People, by empowering all pupils, increasing their motivation and contributing to raising achievement throughout key stages.

It supports pupils in recognising the importance of relationships, teamwork, and the roles and responsibilities of everyone involved in their education. IIP helps pupils to find out why they go to school, about the jobs of everyone in the school and how each person is involved in their education.

Investors in Pupils is based on the following four principles:

1 Commitment – to the development of all its class/school members
2 Review – regularly review the needs of all its class/school members
3 Action – take action to develop class/school members in line with the class/school plan
4 Improvement – understands the difference and development its class/school members can make to class/school performance.

It costs between £250 and £450 to be assessed for the IIP Award, which is dependent on the number of pupils on roll at the school or college. It can take a year to complete the award, but the timescale is flexible.

OFSTED has acknowledged Investors in Pupils in school inspection reports. Greengates Primary School inspection report commented:

> The school's recent gaining of Investors in Pupils award indicates how pupils have a real voice in school.

As a quality mark, IIP does help schools to gather evidence towards meeting the Every Child Matters outcomes, and feeds into the school SEF.

The benefits of participating in the Investors in Pupils award is that:

- it helps to recognise the achievements of whole school or class groups of pupils;
- it contributes to raising standards;
- it involves a range of stakeholders in addition to pupils, e.g. teachers, lunchtime staff, school support staff, governors, parents and carers;
- it builds on existing best practice in schools.

Citizens' juries in schools

Citizens' juries offer the full diversity of pupils in a school's population the opportunity to be constructively involved in developing proposals to inform decision making in improving the Every Child Matters outcomes.

Citizens' juries in schools, as a valuable form of citizenship education, help to fulfil the ECM outcome 'make a positive contribution'. They operate in a similar way to legal court juries, in that they call key witnesses, examine evidence in-depth, give an informed opinion, and make recommendations to decision makers in school, when exploring a real issue or question relevant to pupils' learning, well-being and school life in general.

Examples of issues that a citizens' jury may examine include: revising the Home-School Agreement in light of ECM; developing extended services in school; Building Schools for the Future for ECM/personalisation; and providing a youth club one evening a week in school.

Prior to a citizens' jury taking place in school, a pupil steering group of between 8 and 15 members needs to be established. Members of the steering group may be recruited from the school council as well as from other interested pupils.

The steering group are responsible for:

- planning the citizens' jury;
- producing a detailed timetable for the day's citizens' jury which is sent to jury members and expert witnesses in advance of the event;
- selecting the jury;
- organising and running the citizens' jury on the day;
- recording the jury activities throughout the day;
- presenting the jury's recommendations;
- keeping key stakeholders informed throughout the process;
- following up after the citizens' jury pupil voice activity has occurred, to ensure decision makers take further action.

The steering group do not have any direct influence on the jury's debate or outcomes. It is important that the steering group thank the jury and expert witnesses for their valuable contributions, following the event. All pupils involved in the citizens' jury pupil voice activity, whether they were a member of the steering group or jury or an expert witness, may value being given a certificate to acknowledge and recognise their positive contributions.

The jury comprises 10–12 pupil representatives who may be recruited from the school council, and from pupils directly affected by the issue being examined.

In order for the jury to gather the information they need in relation to making an informed opinion, and offering recommendations to decision makers in school, they will:

- question expert witnesses (i.e. other pupils, teachers, head teacher, governors, parents, local MP or councillor, representatives from other schools, or the local authority Children's Services), allowing up to 20 minutes per expert witness for presentation of evidence and questions;
- brainstorm;
- attend small group or larger group discussions on the ECM issue;
- undertake individual research.

The jury represents the pupils' views and will make its recommendations to decision makers based on secure evidence. The steering group organising the citizens' jury benefits from having a small budget to cover consumables, i.e. flip chart paper, pens, 'post-it' notes, internet access and other ICT equipment, video recorder, refreshments and venue costs, if not held in the school.

Citizens' juries are best held over one day, and it will be important to ensure that pupils who are steering group members or members of the jury can be released from lessons. The recommendations from the jury can be fed back to school decision makers at the end of the day, or alternatively, the steering group may prefer to feedback to the senior leadership team within the next day or two. The outcomes from the event need to be publicised on the school's website, as well as around the school on main notice boards in the reception area, and in classrooms.

The involvement of any members of staff in the citizens' jury is minimal, as they must not directly influence the pupil voice activity. A senior member of staff, or the Citizenship/PSHE Coordinators may help the pupil steering group by:

- securing funding and providing resources
- helping to identify and provide contact information for appropriate expert witnesses
- arranging transport to the venue for the citizens' jury, if held outside school
- negotiating with staff about enabling pupils to miss a day's lessons
- promoting the value of the pupil voice activity among the staff.

The steering group will wish to evaluate the citizens' jury effectiveness, process, impact and outcomes, following the event. They may wish to do this face-to-face with participants, including themselves, or issue a questionnaire for completion. The evaluation needs to focus on what worked well and what could be improved if a future citizens' jury took place. The jury and the steering group members also need to ascertain if they are satisfied with the school decision makers' response, and if there is any further work to be done to move practice forward.

Parent councils and pupil voice

According to the DCSF, every parent matters because:

> Parents are usually the best judges of what children need. They understand their children better than anyone else, and have important insights into what children want.

> (DCSF 2007d: 6)

The government and local authorities know that it is important to listen to what parents have to say, in addition to what their children say, in order that they can act on their views and suggestions to improve and deliver appropriate services to meet their needs.

From 25 May 2007 schools have a duty to take account of the views of parents, and to consider enhancing their current arrangements by setting up a parent council.

A parent council is a body of parents, representing parents, run by parents with the support of the school. Parent members of the parent council usually represent each year group or class in the school, dependent on the phase and size of the school. It is also beneficial for one of the members of the parent council to be parent governor.

Some schools prefer to use the terms Parent Representative Group or Parents' Forum instead of parent council. The parent council does not replace other parent groups such as the Parent Teacher Association (PTA) or the Parent Staff Association (PSA), as they serve different purposes.

The parent council has three distinct purposes:

1 To give parents a voice and increase their active involvement in decision making, fostering a culture of ownership and participation.

2 To develop and strengthen the partnership between the school and parents/carers in order to support and promote pupils' learning and well-being, and bring about change.

3 To act as a critical friend to the school.

Parent councils have an advisory and consultative role. They will have a close working relationship with the school's governing body. They will also have a regular communication route to the school council. The parent council like the school council, both supports the improvement of pupils' learning and well-being in school, and will have valuable views, ideas and information to share. The parent council may invite the chair of the school council to attend relevant meetings, and vice versa.

Further activities

The following questions, based on aspects covered in this chapter, are designed to enable you to discuss and identify positive ways forward, in meeting the challenges and opportunities posed by engaging pupil voice, beyond the school, to reach outside into the wider community, parents/carers and families.

- What informal mechanisms exist in the school that allow pupils to express their thoughts and opinions?
- How are you taking pupils' views into account when designing personalised learning?
- How are pupils participating in decision making and consultation within and beyond the school community?
- How are pupils currently involved in any individual decisions made about their lives?
- How are pupils participating collectively in making decisions about things that affect them?
- How well do pupils take the initiative, work in teams, show responsibility and maturity when making a positive contribution?
- How do pupils share leadership and become involved democratically in school systems?
- How far do pupils feel that the school is a democratic place, and what makes them feel it is?
- How are pupils involved in speaking and advocating for others?
- How do pupils offer support to other pupils and mediate conflict?
- How are pupils volunteering and supporting others in the wider community?
- What do the pupils in your school/class like doing in their spare time, and does anything prevent them from doing constructive activities?
- How are pupils contributing to their local communities?
- What worked well with the citizens' jury?
- What would you do differently or improve if you held another citizens' jury?
- What has been the impact and outcomes for pupils in the whole school, as a result of the recommendations of the citizens' jury?
- How can parents/carers and society in general reconcile children's needs for safety and freedom, and at the same time meet their needs for love and support?
- How have you informed and involved parents/carers in developing and promoting pupil voice?
- How can parents/carers best be involved in supporting pupil voice?
- How does the parent council relate to the school council?
- How do the parent council and the school council share ideas, views and information?
- What opportunities exist for joint events or joint working on Every Child Matters between the parent council and the school council?
- How well do pupils make a positive contribution in the wider community?
- How can we reduce the incidence and impact of peer bullying on pupils?
- How can we provide the kinds of local environment where children and young people feel happy and safe?

- How can we respond to pupils' comments about a lack of leisure opportunities and facilities within their local area?
- How can we respond to children and young people's feelings that they are often mistrusted and stereotyped within their communities, and by society as a whole?
- What opportunities exist for engaging with the wider community?
- Which community issues have pupils identified as a concern to themselves?
- What could pupils do in this school/class to make the local community a better and safer place for them?
- How do pupils in your school/class think they can make a difference to the world around them?

Figure 5.1 Model pupil voice policy

Statement of principle

Every pupil at Leafy Lane School is entitled to have a real say in decisions in school that affect them. As part of personalised learning, all our pupils, as partners in education, play an active role in their learning and school life.

Giving our pupils a 'voice' and 'choice' enables them to play an important role in further developing and improving their school. Through making a positive contribution in their school and within the community, pupils at Leafy Lane School develop into responsible young citizens.

As a whole school approach, pupil voice and participation play a key role in achieving the five Every Child Matters outcomes: be healthy; stay safe; enjoy and achieve; make a positive contribution; and achieve economic well-being.

Aims

Leafy Lane School aims to ensure that:

- an ethos of trust and mutual respect between staff and pupils is promoted whole school;
- staff listen to what pupils have to say;
- pupils are able to express their views in their preferred style of communication;
- pupils feel confident to express and share an opinion without being disadvantaged for having a different view to that of others;
- pupils know how their 'voice' is having a positive impact on improving their learning, well-being and school life in general;
- a good range of opportunities exist for developing pupil 'voice' and participation.

Objectives

Leafy Lane School ensures pupils make a positive contribution by:

- enabling pupils to engage in decision making, to develop positive relationships and self-confidence, and to manage change in their lives;
- providing opportunities for pupils to take responsibility in school;
- providing opportunities for pupils to participate in pupil voice activities both within school and in the local community;
- supporting staff and governors to act as pupil voice advocates;
- feeding back to pupils on the outcomes and impact of their 'voice' in effecting change in school;
- working in partnership with parents/carers to provide information on pupil voice, as well as guidance on how they can support and develop the 'voice' of their child.

Provision

Every Child Matters at Leafy Lane School and that is why all pupils' views, opinions and ideas are valued. Consulting with and involving pupils in decisions about their learning, well-being, aspects of school life and the community helps to prepare them for making wise choices in their lives. In order to ensure pupil 'voice' and participation is fully developed Leafy Lane School offers a good range of opportunities and activities which includes the following:

- School, year and class councils
- Pupil associate governors
- Pupil involvement in key staff appointments
- Pupils as action researchers
- Pupil ambassadors taking visitors on a learning walk around school
- Pupils taking on the roles of peer mentors, peer tutors, peer mediators and counsellors, playground buddies
- Pupil forums, focus groups and working parties
- Annual pupil conference and pupil summit organised and run by the pupils
- Pupil 'Takeover' Day in school where elected pupils run the school
- Pupils as 'change champions' making presentations to staff and the governing body
- Contributing to the completion of the annual pupil survey
- Posting comments on related topics or issues in the pupil voice comment boxes around school
- Maintaining and updating the pupil voice link on the school website and displays on the pupil voice notice board in the school reception area
- Acting as editors and contributors to the school magazine and newsletters

Continued

Relationship with other school policies

The pupil voice policy complements a number of other school policies which include the following:

- Equal opportunities policy
- Every Child Matters policy
- Inclusion policy
- Extended school policy
- Personalised learning policy
- Healthy school policy
- Personal, Social and Health Education Policy (PSHE) and the citizenship policy
- Behaviour and attendance policy
- Safeguarding and child protection policy
- Admissions policy

Coordination

The deputy head teacher, who is the Every Child Matters director, has the responsibility for coordinating pupil voice activities in the school, in addition to ensuring that the pupil voice policy is consistently implemented.

The deputy head teacher monitors and evaluates the effectiveness of the pupil voice policy and practice throughout the school. The deputy head teacher reports on the progress made towards empowering, engaging and enhancing pupil voice to key stakeholders, i.e. head teacher, governing body, staff, school council, parents and carers.

All school staff, including those from external agencies who work with pupils in school, and other extended service providers, all have a responsibility for listening to the views of Leafy Lane pupils, acting on these sensitively, while respecting pupil confidentiality.

Implementation

In order to support the implementation of the school's pupil voice policy and related activities there is:

- provision of governor, staff and pupil training on how to develop pupil voice and participation;
- an agreed understanding of the rights and responsibilities of children and young people among all stakeholders;
- pupil representation in the school's formal management processes;
- an emotionally intelligent school environment which enables pupils to feel confident and safe in sharing their views with others;
- ongoing information and support for parents/carers on pupil voice.

Monitoring and review

The school's pupil voice policy is reviewed annually at the end of each academic year to assess its effectiveness on empowering and enabling pupils to express their views and participate in decision making. Policy evaluation focuses on:

- establishing how far the aims and objectives of the policy have been met;
- how effectively resources have been used to improve pupil voice opportunities;
- the progress pupils have made towards achieving the Every Child Matters outcome 'making a positive contribution';
- seeking feedback from pupils on their view of the impact and outcomes of their 'voice' on effecting change and school improvement;
- seeking the views of staff, parents/carers, governors and other key stakeholders.

In light of all this evidence, the pupil voice policy is revised accordingly.

Ratification of the policy

The school policy on pupil voice was developed through consultation, and was agreed with pupils, parents/carers, staff, governors, and other partners from external agencies and voluntary organisations who work with the school. The governing body approved and ratified the policy in September 2008.

Key dates

Head teacher signature:_____Date:_____

Chair of governors signature:_____Date:_____

Lead school council pupil representatives signature:_____Date:_____

Policy implemented on:_____

Policy review date:_____

Pupil Voice & Participation Charter

This Charter belongs to and was produced by the pupils

Every Child Matters at Leafy Lane School.
All pupils have the right to have a say and take part in all matters and decisions that affect them.

The Charter's Five Principles

1 All adults in school listen to what pupils have to say
2 Pupils are told why their views and ideas have or have not been acted upon
3 Pupils are kept informed about changes and decisions
4 Pupils are guided in how to make positive contributions
5 Pupils are allowed to develop their ideas and make decisions

Date: 30/09/2008

Figure 5.2

6

Pupil Voice in Practice

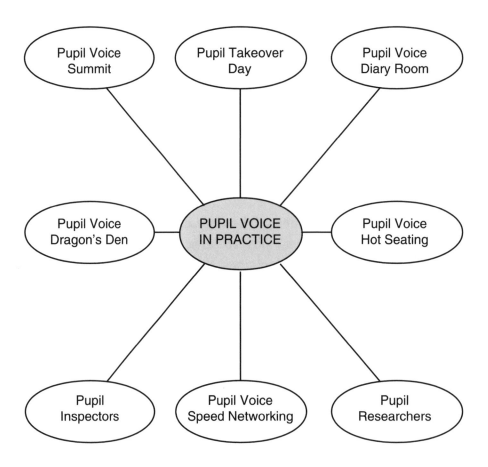

Introduction to the range of approaches and activities

There are a wide range of activities that can provide good quality opportunities for pupils to have a 'voice' and participate in improving and celebrating achievements in the Every Child Matters (ECM) outcomes in schools.

This chapter will offer familiar as well as innovative examples of good practice in pupil voice. These will help to empower pupils to take greater responsibility, and to make positive contributions towards the development of Every Child Matters in school.

The recommended pupil voice activities are all of equal importance. Each activity described caters for the full diversity of pupils, and can readily be tailored or customised according to the school's context. Some pupil voice activities related to ECM may be undertaken across a cluster, network or federation of schools, as well as in an individual educational setting.

Whichever ECM pupil voice activities are selected and utilised, the aims are to:

- ensure that pupils feel they have ownership of the change process and show that their views and opinions are respected
- reassure pupils that their contributions will inform ECM decision making
- add value to the school improvement process for ECM.

Pupil voice activities can be divided into three distinct groups, as illustrated in Table 6.1

Table 6.1 Every Child Matters pupil voice activities

A. Information giving and celebration pupil voice activities	B. Activities seeking pupils' views and ideas	C. Activities informing decision making and promoting responsible pupil leadership
<ul><li>ECM speed networking</li><li>ECM marketplace convention</li><li>ECM annual pupil conference</li><li>ECM pupil ambassadors</li><li>ECM pupil participation champions</li><li>ECM pupil school media and publicity contributors</li></ul>	<ul><li>ECM diary room</li><li>ECM pupil summit</li><li>ECM School I'd like competition</li><li>ECM enterprise and innovation road show</li><li>ECM pupil researchers</li></ul>	<ul><li>ECM hot seating</li><li>ECM pupil takeover day</li><li>Pupils supporting the recruitment and appointment of staff for ECM</li><li>Pupil shadowing ECM governor for a day</li><li>ECM pupils' radio call-in show</li><li>ECM pupil inspectors</li></ul>

Every Child Matters speed networking

Pupils from a class/form group, year group or from a Key Stage can participate in Every Child Matters speed networking. Ideally a group of pupils are nominated to organise and run the speed networking session.

Five tables are set out with six or eight chairs at each table. Pens and 'post-it' notes are available on the tables. Each table takes a different Every Child Matters outcome, which is displayed on a table card. Each pupil at the table has two minutes to tell the other pupils about a positive ECM experience or pupil voice activity/action related to the specific ECM outcome.

During the 12- or 16-minute networking session for each table, pupils jot down on the 'post-it' notes anything they find interesting, new, or further questions they wish to pursue, which arise from listening to their peers. All the pupils' comments are anonymous. The 'post-it' notes are placed on flip chart sheets which are displayed on the wall or board, beside each table.

After 12 or 16 minutes a bell is rung and all pupils move to join a new table. This process is repeated until all five ECM outcomes have been covered. Teachers and teaching assistants can be available during the activity. Their role is to act as observers who encourage pupil participation, but who do not inhibit their contributions.

A total time of between 1 hour and 1 hour 20 minutes is allowed for the activity. Following the speed networking event all comments are collated for each ECM outcome and typed up in a report of findings which can be put on the school's website, as well as being fed back to pupils, governors, staff and other key stakeholders.

Every Child Matters marketplace convention

This activity is organised by a group of pupils who may be members of the school council, or a representative from each form or class group who form the organising events committee. They agree and plan the event. The event is an annual activity, whereby each class or year group have a display stand and a stall which describes and illustrates the range of ECM collective activities and achievements within their class or year group.

In addition, the organising committee of pupils invite staff representatives from the school's Personalised Learning and ECM Well-Being Team, as well as other professionals from external agencies (education, health and social care) to provide a display and stall describing their work with pupils in the school to improve the ECM outcomes.

Displays may be static or interactive, making use of multimedia technology to deliver ongoing short presentations, e.g. PowerPoint, DVD snapshots of ECM in action. Pupils may also produce their own information leaflets or resources for their marketplace stall.

The event is ideally held from 4pm to 6pm at the end of the school day. This will enable parents/carers, members of the local community, and those visiting from other schools and the local authority children's services, to attend the event.

The aim of the activity is to inform those visiting the event about how the ECM outcomes are developing throughout the school. The event can act as a showcase to publicise pupil voice in action and good practice in ECM. The event is fairly economical to run, with the majority of costs covering refreshments and display resources.

Snapshots of the entire event can be recorded during the evening and posted on the school's website and can contribute to evidence to submit for any external Every Child Matters awards, as well as supporting the school's SEF.

Every Child Matters annual pupil conference

This is an example of a high profile showcase day event, where a pupil committee organises and agrees the programme and the format of the day conference. Table 6.2 provides a useful planning framework for pupils.

Pupils can decide whether to commission an external keynote speaker and workshop presenters, as well as using in-house local deliverers. This activity could be an event that a group of local schools in a cluster hold collectively. The pupils are allocated a budget for the event, which they are responsible for managing and spending wisely.

Pupil representatives are invited from cluster or partner schools, as well as the ECM governor(s), a member of the senior leadership team, the PSHE Coordinator, and representatives from Children's Services.

Table 6.2 Pupil's Every Child Matters Event Planning Sheet

Lead organiser of the event: _____

Event title: _____

Date of event: _____

Start time: _____   End time: _____

Event venue: _____

Aims of the event: _____

_____

_____

Programme (nature of activities): _____

_____

_____

_____

_____

_____

Audience for event: _____

_____

Maximum numbers:

_____

Health, safety and accessibility arrangements:

_____

_____

_____

Resources required for the event:

ICT:

_____

Room layout:

_____

Resources for tables:

_____

Refreshment requirements:

On arrival: _____

Mid-morning: _____

Lunchtime: _____

Mid-afternoon: _____

Entrance fee: _____

Concessions: _____

Event publicity: Flyers ☐ Letter ☐ Website ☐

No. of pupil helpers for event: _____

Roles of pupil helpers at event: _____

_____

_____

_____

Event total budget: £ _____

Advertising costs: £ _____

Equipment hire: £ _____

Venue costs: £ _____

Table 6.2 Continued

Refreshment costs: £ _____

Administration costs: £ _____

Speaker/Presenter's fees: £ _____

Event evaluation

Feedback methods: evaluation sheet ☐ post-its ☐

What did delegates think of the event overall?

_____
_____
_____

How will you feedback the outcomes of the event, and to whom?

_____
_____
_____

Event aims achieved: YES ☐ NO ☐

What have you learned from the experience?

_____
_____
_____
_____

What would you do differently next time to improve the event?

_____
_____
_____
_____

The workshops provided during the day could focus on topics that the pupils themselves identify as valuable for further developing their ECM know-how. For example, workshops for pupils attending the conference could cover: counselling skills; how to organise and manage meetings; action research skills; team-building skills; leadership skills; conflict resolution and negotiation skills; public speaking and debating skills.

Any external keynote speakers will be inspirational, and act as an ambassador or champion for children. The venue would be local within one of the partner schools, or in a local authority venue or in a local hotel with conference facilities. Snapshots of the one-day conference would be filmed and available on the participating schools' websites.

Every Child Matters pupil ambassadors

Pupils taking on the role of ECM pupil ambassadors promote and publicise to visitors, new and prospective pupils, the school's and pupils' achievements in relation to pupil voice and participation in ECM policy and practice.

They are on hand to take visitors and pupils on an ECM learning walk tour of the school. These pupils are able to answer questions and describe in detail the ECM work and achievements on display, or taking place on the day visit. Visitors and new pupils see pupil participation and ECM in action, as part of everyday practice in reality, rather than as being one-off showcase events. This role is acknowledged in the pupils' personal development portfolios. ECM pupil ambassadors feel a sense of pride and valued in taking on this important role.

Every Child Matters pupil participation champions

Nominated pupils who undertake this wide-ranging position of responsibility at a class or year group level play a key role in ensuring that pupils' involvement remains high on the school's ECM agenda. They also provide advice on pupils' active involvement and participation in contributing to ECM policy and practice to the school leadership team, and to the local authority, when requested.

In order to undertake the role effectively there are certain personal qualities pupils require. These include:

- ability to listen to other pupils' viewpoints and ideas
- being open, approachable, trustworthy and respect confidentiality
- having good communication skills
- ability to engage with pupils of all ages, abilities, and from a range of cultural and social backgrounds
- ability to remain impartial and non-judgemental
- ability to use a range of approaches to enable pupils of different ages to express their views and ideas
- being committed to representing the views of other pupils.

The main duties for the role of pupil participation champion include:

- ensuring that pupil voice and active participation is considered in relation to all decisions that have an impact on them
- ensuring the full diversity of pupils have access to pupil voice and participation structures and procedures
- ensuring pupils' views are included and presented appropriately to inform Every Child Matters decision making in school
- ensuring they meet with pupils in their class and/or year group regularly
- ensuring action takes place and/or feedback is given, as a result of pupils' sharing their views and ideas about Every Child Matters
- ensuring resources available for the role are used effectively
- meeting regularly with other pupil participation champions in school
- keeping up-to-date with school and local issues relating to Every Child Matters well-being outcomes, pupil learning, and pupil lifestyle issues
- undertaking relevant training to enhance and further develop the role of the pupil participation champion, when required.

ECM pupil school media and publicity contributors

Pupils as volunteers on the school's media and publicity team take responsibility for producing and contributing to the production of the in-house ECM newsletter and information leaflets for parents/carers, new pupils and for external professionals seeking information about the school's ECM policy and practice.

The pupils have ownership and make decisions about what is featured each term in the ECM school newsletter. They are responsible for researching in-school articles on best practice relating to ECM outcomes.

Pupils take it in turn to be the editor, photographers and investigative journalists covering each of the ECM outcomes.

Feedback is requested from those receiving an ECM newsletter or information leaflet, on any items they would wish to feature in future editions.

Name:

Welcome to Leafy Lane School

Where Every Child Matters and has a Voice and Choice

Who is responsible for Pupil Voice and Every Child Matters?

The Deputy Headteacher, who is the Director for Every Child Matters in the school, is responsible for Pupil Voice and Every Child Matters.

Share your views with the Deputy Headteacher

Speak Out now

PUPIL VOICE AND CHOICE HAVE YOUR SAY

www.leafylane@ecmvoice.sch.uk

www.11MILLION.org.uk
www.everychildmatters.gov.uk

PUPIL VOICE AND EVERY CHILD MATTERS

Introduction

Leafy Lane School is a happy, welcoming place in which to learn, make new friends and have a say about your learning, well being and school life in general.

As a new pupil at Leafy Lane School, where Every Child Matters, you will be healthy, safe, enjoy and achieve, make a positive contribution, and achieve economic well being.

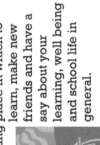

Reach for the stars at Leafy Lane School to fulfill your potential

The new ideas and interests you have will be valued and will help Leafy Lane School to become even more Every Child Matters-friendly.

This leaflet tells you what you can expect from school to support your learning and well being.

In the classroom

You will find the following:

The Every Child Matters five outcomes displayed

An agreed whole class Every Child Matters target

Your own personal target for Every Child Matters

A pupil 'voice' area where the class achievements can be celebrated

A class representative to listen to your views

A School Council representative to take class views to the School Council Meetings

Internet access to the school's website with links to the pupils forum and information centre.

A pupil comment box

Pupil voice and Every Child Matters
Participation in decision making

Who can help you?

Class teacher and teaching assistant

Learning Mentor and Pupils Personal Adviser

Pupil Mentors, Pupil Tutors, Pupil Counsellors, Playground Buddies

School Nurse

Mid-day lunchtime assistants

Family Liaison worker

Other adults from Education, Health and Social Care Services, who work in the school

PUPIL VOICE AND CHOICE HAVE YOUR SAY

www.leafylane@ecmvoice.sch.uk

Figure 6.1

Every Child Matters diary room

Setting up a 'Big Brother' style ECM video diary room is a good interactive and exciting way to consult with pupils on aspects of Every Child Matters. Dependent on the age and technological skills of the pupils, a small group of older pupils could be nominated to organise, run and film the diary room event. Alternatively, schools are likely to wish to commission an external professional filming team to record the event. Pupils will, however, be responsible for planning and devising the questions on ECM for the diary room, as well as advising on the room layout.

A member of staff will oversee but not interfere in the diary room event. They will be responsible for seeking written permission from the parents and carers of pupils participating in the event. In addition, they will also ensure ethical and legal guidelines regarding filmed consultation with children and young people are followed.

The pupils leading the diary room activity will prepare in advance crib cards which contain a broad range of questions for the pupils in the diary room to answer, on issues of relevance to the Every Child Matters outcomes.

Examples of questions for crib cards could include the following:

- *What aspects of Every Child Matters worry or concern pupils in school?*
- *What are pupils happy and unhappy about concerning Every Child Matters in school?*
- *What more could be done to improve the leadership, management and organisation of ECM in school?*
- *What could pupils do themselves to make the ECM outcomes better in school?*
- *How would you wish to participate in ECM pupil voice activities?*
- *Who else from within or outside school could support improving the ECM outcomes in school for pupils?*
- *How could parents/carers of pupils contribute to supporting and improving the ECM outcomes in school?*
- *What more could be done in school to enable pupils to keep healthy, be safe, enjoy and achieve, make a positive contribution and enjoy economic well-being?*

A further enticement to encourage pupils to participate in the ECM diary room pupil voice activity would be to offer a raffle ticket for entry to a free prize draw at the end of the session. Prizes could be donated by external sponsors, local businesses, in the form of vouchers for books, sports equipment, cinema vouchers, a free family meal voucher at a local restaurant, or high street store gift vouchers.

The diary room ideally runs for half a day or a full day, depending on how many pupils the school wishes to consult with. This type of activity could be run simultaneously alongside a pupil summit on ECM.

A report of findings and an edited CD of the diary room pupil interviews will be produced which will be presented to governors, the senior leadership team, staff, pupils, parents and carers and external professionals working with the school. If a group of schools within a cluster group participate collectively in the ECM diary room, then the other participating schools would receive recorded evidence of the event.

Overall, the findings from the diary room activity help to inform future school ECM policy and practice, as well as demonstrating to pupils that their views really are valued, listened to and acted upon.

Every Child Matters pupil summit

This ECM pupil voice activity is usually organised by a school's or cluster of schools' senior leadership team for a year group or Key Stage. Alternatively, it may be run by the local authority to inform an ECM priority on their Children and Young People's Plan (CYPP). The event could be hosted by a school, or held in an external venue.

The purpose of the half-day activity is to enable five or six nominated pupils from each participating school, accompanied by a senior member of staff and/or the ECM governor, to share their views on what children and young people wish to see improved in relation to the ECM outcomes.

The event organiser may be a member of a school's senior leadership team, the PSHE coordinator, or a local authority officer. A Power Point presentation describing the aims and expected outcomes for the event is a valuable opener to the pupil summit. A series of questions and activities are prepared in advance, which will help to inform future decision making within schools or in the local authority Children's Services.

An example of an activity pupils are likely to undertake at the summit may be:

> *In order of priority, what five things would you ask the head teacher, or the LA Director of Children's Services to do, in order to make the Every Child Matters five outcomes better for pupils?*

Pupils would discuss this question/task within their school table groups, and the accompanying member of staff and/or the ECM school governor would act as facilitators to the pupils' discussion, but in no way lead or dominate the dialogue.

The collective and agreed responses to the task would be written up on flip chart paper, identifying the name of the school, but not the name of any pupils or staff. The importance of confidentiality and anonymous responses must be emphasised by the organiser and presenter at the pupil summit. Each table in turns feeds back to all the participants at the summit their five ECM priorities. The lead presenter at the event will identify congruence, similarities and new ideas from the activity, summarising the findings and praising pupils for their valuable contributions. This first activity usually takes up to 45 minutes including feedback.

A refreshment break is advisable following this first task, which provides an opportunity for staff, governors and pupils to network with those from other schools and to look again at the schools' responses to the first task.

The second task requires school staff and ECM governors to move to another school table. They will introduce themselves to a new group of pupils. The pupils will introduce themselves to the new adult joining their school table. Task 2 could take the following format:

> *In partnership with the headteacher or Director of Children's Services, how would the pupils help him/her to meet, achieve and make the five identified school ECM priorities and actions from Task 1 actually happen?*

Once again, pupils discuss this task with their school peers at the table. The adults again act as facilitators of discussion, but do not inhibit pupils' views and ideas. The pupils write each ECM priority or activity from Task 1 on a separate piece of flip chart paper, and under each ECM priority they produce a bullet point list of actions and solutions for meeting the priority. Once again the presenter for the day asks each group in turn to feed back at least one or two suggested solutions or actions from Task 2 to all the participants in the room. These solutions to improving ECM outcomes are again displayed on flip chart paper on the wall for other participants to view.

The session concludes with an overall summing up and thanks from the lead presenter for the summit. The findings are typed up and published on each school's website and/or on the LA school intranet. The presenter emphasises that there will be a follow-up second pupil summit at the beginning of the new school academic year to see how schools and the LA have acted on the views of pupils to make improvements in Every Child Matters.

The pupil summit has cost implications for individual schools, clusters of schools and for the local authority (LA). The budget for the event will need to cover resources for the pupils, e.g. a 'goody' bag comprising a pen, highlighter, a pack of 'post-it' notes and a ruler, mouse mat or drinks coaster. In addition, there will be venue hire costs which cover refreshments, any flip chart paper and pens, and ICT equipment.

The Every Child Matters 'School I'd Like' competition for pupils

This activity provides an excellent opportunity for pupils who find it difficult to express their views orally, to illustrate their ideal ECM school using image-based techniques in the format of a hand-drawn or computer-produced illustration, mind map, or multimedia montage of photographs or artwork. There would need to be a deadline date set for entries to be submitted and this needs to be strictly adhered to. Pupils must produce their ideas for an 'ECM School I'd Like' themselves, unaided by any adult support.

Entries to the competition would be judged by an external 'critical friend' who knows the school. Prizes would be awarded in the form of gift vouchers to pupils winning in their category, e.g. year group, Key Stage, age group.

Every Child Matters enterprise and innovation roadshow 'Dragon's Den'

This type of ECM activity is best organised and held between a cluster, network or federation of local schools. The local authority (LA) may sponsor the event in partnership with local businesses and services. A panel of representatives from local businesses and Children's Services will judge the pupils' ECM business ideas and initiatives related to improving any of the five outcomes for children and young people from a number of schools.

Similar to the 'Dragon's Den' concept, pupils must present to the panel of judges the benefits and cost-effectiveness of their initiative, along with a demonstration of their idea/invention, which is designed to improve or further develop an ECM outcome for pupils in their school.

Pupils may need pre-tutoring as to how to devise and present a business plan from staff or local entrepreneurs, who are willing to give their expertise free of charge. These supporting adults must be impartial, and be unknown to any of the judges on the panel.

Where the pupils' initiatives are considered to be worthy of promotion and sponsorship, and have a wider market viability in schools and educational settings across the LA, these will be acknowledged through a school award and local publicity. The pupils will also see their invention, idea or initiative put into production and used in schools locally.

Every Child Matters pupil researchers

Pupils can be independent or co-researchers with teachers to explore aspects of Every Child Matters in school. Pupils should take ownership of the process by agreeing the focus for the ECM research with the head teacher or the deputy head teacher, conducting the research and reporting back on findings. Pupils as researchers in ECM will require training for the role, which can be

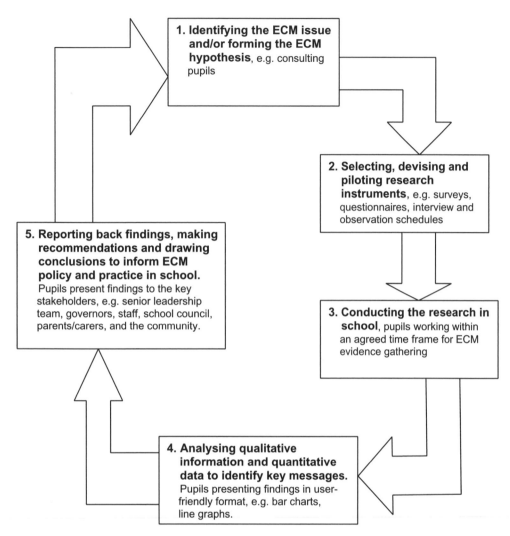

Figure 6.2 Stages in the process of pupils as researchers on ECM

delivered by staff in school, or purchased from the local authority or from an independent training company. The nature of the training will need to focus on developing the following skills: wording questions and designing surveys, questionnaires and interview schedules; how to interview and observe practice; how to analyse, interpret and present evidence; and how to draw conclusions and make relevant recommendations for improving ECM.

A good starting-point for pupils to identify Every Child Matters aspects to explore further in school would be for them to answer two initial questions:

1   *What isn't working well in school in relation to Every Child Matters outcomes?*
2   *What could pupils in partnership with staff and other stakeholders do to find a solution to improve the ECM issue?*

Some suggested ECM issues that pupils may wish to explore further include:

- *Pupils want to explore how to increase opportunities in school to help them develop enterprising behaviour.*
- *Pupils want teachers to put the 'fun' back in the curriculum so that they can enjoy their learning more.*
- *Pupils want to explore how to get more opportunities in school to learn about how to deal with peer pressure, change and challenges in their lives.*
- *Pupils wish to explore how teachers can help them to achieve economic well-being in Key Stage 1 and Key Stage 2.*

- *Pupils want more support in school to enable them to cope with exam stress.*
- *Pupils think the school needs to do more to inform parents/carers and the community about Every Child Matters.*

Pupils as researchers would explore one of these issues over a term, and report their findings, conclusions and recommendations back to the senior leadership team, governors, staff and pupils. Pupils also like to see their recommendations acted upon fairly quickly, and it would be envisaged that some change or action for improvement would take place in six to nine months' time, or at least a guarantee be given to the pupil ECM research team that there will be a priority on the forthcoming revised school improvement plan.

The benefits of pupils leading and undertaking school-based research on an aspect of Every Child Matters are as follows:

- they feel respected, listened to and taken seriously by adults in school;
- they see their research can influence improvement and lead to change;
- a climate of trust and openness is established, where ECM talk becomes part of everyday practice;
- enables research skills to transfer across the curriculum;
- enhances teamwork within a school's learning community;
- enhances self-confidence and communication skills.

Every Child Matters hot seating

Pupils from a class sit in a half circle on chairs at the front of the room, facing the head teacher, or deputy head teacher, who is the director or manager for ECM in the school. Alternatively, pupils may wish to hot seat the school's ECM governor.

One pupil from the class stands up and explains the objectives of the activity to the class and to the adult being hot seated on ECM. Examples of questions pupils may ask could be:

- *'We need to clarify what the whole school vision is for Every Child Matters';*
- *'What will Every Child Matters look like in Leafy Lane School in five years' time?';*
- *'What is your first priority for improving Every Child Matters outcomes for pupils in school?';*
- *'How do you see pupils in school contributing to making Every Child Matters outcomes better?'*

The class teacher acts as an observer, who records the activity on film. They also remind the pupils of the ground rules about hot seating, e.g. to make no comments on the questions asked or on the answers given by the person in the hot seat, except to ask a further relevant question.

The advantages of hot seating for Every Child Matters ensures that more pupils within a class have access to the same information about ECM, irrespective of ability, in an appealing and realistic way. Pupils are able to determine what information they receive on ECM, giving them ownership in managing hot seating as part of the learning process.

The hot seat interview can take between 15 and 20 minutes. As a follow-up activity to the exercise, pupils could be asked to research an aspect of ECM arising from the hot seat interview, and to bring their findings back to a second hot seat interview with the same senior leaders at the end of term.

Every Child Matters pupils' 'takeover' day

This is a one-day activity suitable for primary and secondary schools. Ideally it is held on the same day as the England Children's Commissioner's national Takeover Day. The first national Takeover Day took place on Friday 23 November 2007.

The aim of the day is to give pupils an insight into potential future careers as well as a taste of power in schools' business and politics, by their taking over adult jobs for a day.

Pupils are asked by the senior leadership team to apply for particular jobs relating to Every Child Matters in the school's children's workforce. This can include being the ECM manager, the headteacher, the ECM governor, a leading TA for ECM, a lunchtime supervisor, office administrator, or site manager. Pupils may also take on the role of class teachers delivering a PSHE lesson on Every Child Matters.

Pupils are interviewed for each post, and have an opportunity to shadow the relevant adult before they actually take on the role on the takeover day. The number of pupils who participate in the activity is dependent on the size, phase, and context of the school.

The range of experiences the pupils undertake can vary from taking a whole school assembly, to leading a staff briefing, to delivering a presentation to staff and governors at a meeting, to taking a lesson, supervising pupils at lunchtime, undertaking administrative tasks in the school office, and meeting with the school council to listen to pupils' ECM views and issues.

Pupils need to have the opportunity to feed back to the adults whose roles they undertook for the day their views and opinions about the job they did.

Pupils supporting the recruitment and appointment of ECM staff

Some schools are already involving pupils at various stages in recruiting and appointing staff who have an important role in Every Child Matters in school. For example, pupils may be involved in recruiting and appointing learning mentors, pupil counsellors, teaching assistants, ECM director, manager or coordinator.

The degree to which pupils are involved in and understand the process will be dependent on their age, maturity, and the pre-training the pupils receive to prepare them for undertaking such an important role. The key elements of a pupil training programme for recruiting and appointing staff should include:

- how to write job advertisements, job descriptions and person specifications
- how to shortlist
- how to formulate interview questions
- interviewing techniques and skills
- how to record observations and candidates' responses
- listening skills
- confidentiality
- equal opportunities
- decision making.

Pupil participation may include: helping to produce a job description; providing suggestions as to what to include in an information pack to applicants; proposing questions for the school council to ask shortlisted candidates at interview; observing applicants undertaking their role in school, in partnership with a member of the senior leadership team; taking prospective candidates on an ECM learning walk around the school.

The school council may request that candidates deliver a presentation to them on how they will ensure that Every Child Matters in their school.

Suggested questions that pupils on the school council may wish to ask prospective candidates during interview could be as follows:

- *How would you consult pupils in your class?*
- *How would you encourage pupils in you class to listen to the views of others?*
- *How would you encourage pupils in your class to give their points of view?*
- *What three essential qualities do you consider to be essential from a pupil's viewpoint, to enable them to achieve good ECM outcomes?*
- *Why do you think you could make a real difference to pupil voice and Every Child Matters in this school?*
- *How would you help pupils in your role to achieve successful Every Child Matters well-being outcomes?*
- *How would you help pupils in this school to achieve economic well-being?*
- *How would you explain to a pupil that their view or idea cannot be acted upon at present?*

Involving pupils in the recruitment and appointment of ECM staff is crucial, particularly as relating to children and young people is such an important aspect of any role in the school's children's workforce.

Pupil Every Child Matters governor for a day

Although any pupil under 18 can become an associate governor, this limits the number of pupils who can gain an insight into school governance. In order to broaden the pupils' experience of governance in school, the head teacher in consultation with the governing body may decide how they could offer a number of pupils such an opportunity without becoming an associate governor.

Observing and shadowing the role of the governor responsible for Every Child Matters in the school may offer pupils the ideal opportunity, particularly if more than one governor takes responsibility for ECM. For example, five different governors may have responsibility for one of the ECM outcomes. This pupil voice ECM governance activity could become part of the national Takeover Day in school.

Pupils would apply to become an ECM governor for a day and, if successful following an interview, they would shadow the relevant governor(s) in school for a day. This may involve them observing a lesson with the ECM governor; attending a meeting with the ECM director or manager; attending a governing body meeting or school council meeting, where Every Child Matters is an agenda item, and presenting pupils' collective views on ECM.

Every Child Matters pupils' local radio call-in show

This innovative pupil voice activity would entail a nominated representative group of pupils from the school's ECM Pupil Community Task Force seeking permission from the head teacher to organise and run a sponsored local radio station call-in show for listeners about improving the Every Child Matters outcomes for children and young people in the local community.

The pupils would be responsible for preparing and scripting their own set of questions to ask listeners on the topic. These would be shared with the school's senior leadership team as well as with the radio presenter before pupils go live 'on air' on the radio.

Suggested questions pupils may wish to ask daytime radio listeners on ECM in the local community for children and young people include:

- *How could the local community be made safer for children and young people to enjoy safe outdoor play and other productive leisure activities out of school hours?*
- *What could members of the local community do to ensure that children and young people are not exposed to unhealthy leisure pursuits?*

- *How can adults in the local community take greater responsibility in safeguarding children and young people from the negative pressures of consumerism?*

Seeking sponsorship, support and guidance from a local daytime radio presenter to host the pupils' ECM call-in session will be a necessity. The school will need to commission and fund the pupils' transportation to and from the studios of the local radio station, if they do not have their own mini-bus available.

Every Child Matters pupil inspectors

This forward-thinking pupil voice activity entails five nominated pupils per Key Stage, each undertaking a mini-inspection trail in the school to evaluate the quality, effectiveness and impact of one of the five Every Child Matters (ECM) outcomes, from a pupil's perspective.

Ideally, the activity would be carried out prior to a forthcoming OFSTED inspection, over one or two school days. Pupils, as ECM inspectors, will require pre-training for the role. This training should cover the following aspects: code of conduct for inspection; confidentiality; observing lessons and other ECM pupil activities; conducting interviews; sampling pupils' work and achievements in ECM; simple ECM data analysis; and report writing.

The ECM pupil inspectors will require a simplified 'child-friendly' version of the OFSTED inspection schedule criteria for gathering first-hand evidence and judging the quality of ECM outcomes. A senior member of staff within the school will need to coordinate this pupil participation activity. They will need to coach and mentor the ECM pupil inspectors, and support them while they undertake this role, e.g. by carrrying out paired observations with ECM pupil inspectors.

It may be a valuable experience for pupil inspectors to shadow a member of the senior leadership team undertaking a similar school evaluation trail, before they conduct their own pupil ECM inspection trail, in-house.

Any external service providers from education, health or social care delivering extended service provision to pupils on the school site will need to be made aware that they may be interviewed by an ECM pupil inspector, who will be seeking evidence on the impact of their interventions in improving the ECM outcomes for pupils. ECM pupil inspectors would not observe any pupils receiving individual support such as counselling or personal health care, as confidentiality is paramount.

The evidence ECM pupil inspectors gather would need to be written up for each Every Child Matters outcome and Key Stage. The ECM pupil inspectors will need to nominate a lead pupil inspector, to bring all the findings together in one report. The ECM pupil inspection team would meet up to discuss and agree the overall findings, and identify ECM areas that require further improvement. The team would agree an OFSTED grade for each ECM outcome. The lead ECM pupil inspector would feed back the overall findings to the senior leadership team and the chair of governors. The school leadership team and the chair of governors would have the opportunity to ask the ECM lead pupil inspector to clarify any issues arising from the report feedback.

This is an excellent activity for informing the school's self-evaluation form (SEF), Part A, Sections 2 and 4. OFSTED would welcome such an innovative approach to engaging pupil voice and participation.

7

Evaluating the Impact and Outcomes of Pupil Voice

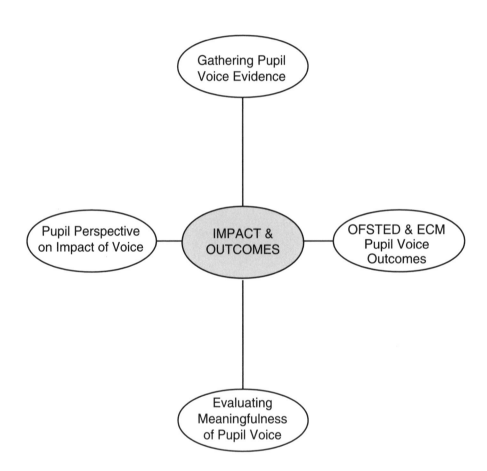

This final chapter will provide a range of practical resources to enable senior leaders and managers, classroom practitioners, and those from external agencies providing services to pupils in schools, to gather robust evidence in relation to documenting the impact of pupil voice activities on outcomes for children and young people.

The CfBT/NFER research into pupil voice and school improvement (Halsey *et al.* 2007) identified the following key issues in relation to evaluating the impact of pupil voice.

- Schools and staff involved with engaging pupil voice need to direct their attention to the outcomes stemming from the activity.
- More systematic, routine and in-depth evaluation of the impact of pupil voice and participation in schools is required.
- Where pupils are involved in decision making and change, schools must ensure that the outcomes of their involvement are properly evaluated and recorded.
- The evaluation should be comprehensive, inviting contributions from the pupils themselves about the impact on them personally, and the advantages of their involvement.
- The impact arising from pupils' involvement and participation should be tracked in the longer term in order to obtain a full picture of their contributions.
- Although pupil voice is viewed as an engine for school improvement, it is important to indicate and document how such improvement came about as a result of pupil voice activities.
- An external impartial adult should be engaged to support pupils in evaluating the impact and effectiveness of services delivered by education, health and social care to pupils in schools.

The deputy head teacher Annabel Kay at Lawrence Sheriff School, Rugby, in Warwickshire commented:

> Student voice is a major resource that we neglect at our peril. If we spent just a fraction of our resources on improving the way we listen to students, the impact upon the education system in the UK could be more profound than any school improvement project we have yet seen.
>
> (QCA 2006: 2)

The chapter offers a range of evaluation resources. This enables classroom practitioners and school leaders to choose whether they use all or only some of the models provided, according to the school context. The main intention is to avoid a 'death by audit' approach, and to offer tools that only collect meaningful evidence on the impact of pupil voice.

The evidence not only contributes to internal evaluation processes, e.g. SEF, but also provides good-quality, robust and telling evidence of the impact of pupil voice to external professionals, e.g. OFSTED inspectors, School Improvement Partner (SIP), local authority officers.

Senior leaders who specifically wish to evaluate the impact of their school council may wish to access the School Councils UK's excellent resource *Activity Guide 04 Evaluating Your School Council* (2005a), which can be downloaded free from the website: www.schoolcouncils.org.

The chapter concludes with further activities, which promote further thinking and reflection about the effectiveness, quality of impact and future developments for pupil voice within the educational setting.

Evidence OFSTED inspectors will seek on pupil voice

School leaders and class/subject teachers will be expected to contribute telling evidence to the schools' self evaluation form (SEF) in response to the following questions:

(a) SEF Part A, Section 2: Views of learners, parents/carers and other stakeholders:

- **What are the views of learners and how do you know?**

  2a How do you gather the views of learners, such as those accessing additional services?
     How often do you do this?
     How do you ensure the impartiality of the information?

  2b What do the views of learners tell you about the learners' standards, personal development
     and well-being, and the quality of your provision?

  2c How do you share with parents/carers and other stakeholders the collated findings about
     pupils' views?

  2d Can you give examples of action you have taken based on the views of learners, with an
     evaluation of the effectiveness of what you did?

(b) SEF Part A Section 4d: How well do learners make a positive contribution to the community?

   Learners' understanding of their rights and responsibilities, and those of others.
   How well learners express their views and take part in community activities both within and
   beyond the school.

How OFSTED inspectors will gather pupil voice evidence

- Documentary evidence from the school's SEF
- Documentary evidence from the pupil voice school policy, Pupils' Charter, school mission
  statement, school profile, school prospectus, home–school agreement, induction information
  for new pupils
- Direct first-hand evidence during inspection by talking to pupils informally and formally, i.e.
  in a school council meeting
- Observing pupil voice activities in action, e.g. a school council meeting, a school assembly,
  pupil forum, citizens' jury
- Observing snapshots of lessons across the curriculum, and in particular, PSHE, Citizenship,
  RE, after-school activities
- Sampling pupils' work and achievements
- Talking to other stakeholders, e.g. governors, parents/carers, and staff about how they get to
  hear about pupils' views on school matters, and if they know the actions taken as a result of this.

Further activities

The following questions, based on aspects covered in this chapter, are designed to enable you to
discuss and identify positive ways forward in monitoring and evaluating the impact of pupil voice.

- Overall, what has been the impact of dialogue with pupils regarding Every Child Matters from
  the pupils' perspective?
- What has been the impact of pupil voice in the ECM staff recruitment process?
- How far are pupil voice activities democratic? How do you know? Where is your evidence?
- What has worked well and what has not worked as well in relation to pupil voice activities?
- What were the three most successful examples of pupil voice activities in the school, and why
  were they particularly successful in terms of impact and outcomes?
- What is the evidence telling us about what we believe and value in engaging pupil voice?
- How has pupil voice impacted on improving the ECM outcomes?
- What has been the overall outcome of pupils having genuine influence over key decisions that
  affect them?
- In what ways are you monitoring the impact of pupil voice?
- What impact has pupil voice and participation had on decision making and school change?

- What are the views of pupils telling you about the strengths and weaknesses of the school, particularly in relation to ECM outcomes?
- What can be learned from the outcomes and impact of pupil voice in this school?
- What has been the impact of pupil voice and participation in the production of information materials and resources in school?
- How do the outcomes from your pupil voice activities compare with those in other local schools?

Evaluating the impact of pupil voice on ECM outcomes

Introduction

The views of pupils are important to the head teacher and staff in school.
Please answer the following questions honestly.
All responses are anonymous.
We only ask you to indicate which year group and form group you are in, and whether you are a girl or a boy.

Year group [ ]   Form [ ]   Girl [ ]   Boy [ ]

Questions

1. Which have been the best ways for giving your views on Every Child Matters in school?

2. How do you know whether your views and ideas have been listened to and acted upon by the head teacher, staff and governors in the school?

3. Who in school tells you if your views or ideas have not been acted upon?

4. What reason is given for not acting upon your views and ideas?

5. Do you consider that your views about Every Child Matters in school have really helped to improve outcomes for pupils?

   YES [ ]   NO [ ]
   If yes, state how your views helped to improve Every Child Matters in school.

6. Who is the first adult in school you trust, to share your views and ideas with?

7. Do you feel you are always asked to give your views on Every Child Matters topics that are of interest to the head teacher and staff in the school, rather than what pupils want to find out about the topic?

   YES [ ]   NO [ ]

8. Are there any other ways in which your views, opinions and ideas on Every Child Matters could be gathered in school?

Thank you for taking the time to answer these questions.
Please post this survey in the post box located in the main school entrance.
The results of this survey will be published in a week's time in all form rooms.

Figure 7.1

Evaluating pupil voice whole school or in the classroom

1. How many ideas and views of pupils in relation to improving Every Child Matters (ECM) outcomes were acted upon this academic year?

2. Which was the best pupil ECM idea that had the most impact?

3. How many pupils' ideas and views in relation to ECM were not acted upon?

4. Briefly outline the reasons why the pupils' ECM ideas were not acted upon.

5. Were there any pupil groups whose voice was under-represented?

6. What action will you take to ensure pupil voice activities are more inclusive, engaging the full diversity of pupils?

7. How many pupils as a percentage of the class, or whole school pupil population, expressed a view and participated in change for ECM?

8. In what ways did you gather pupil voice?

9. What was the most effective way of engaging pupil voice?

10. What do you consider to be the main advantages to pupils in being able to express their views and ideas on improving ECM outcomes this academic year?

11. What barriers have prevented you from further enhancing and developing pupil 'voice' at:
    (a) whole school level?

    (b) classroom level?

    (c) community level?

12. What strategies and initiatives will you put in place next academic year to remove pupil voice barriers at:
    (a) whole school level?

    (b) classroom level?

    (c) community level?

Figure 7.2

Table 7.1 Model framework for evaluating the impact of pupil voice on improving the Every Child Matters outcomes*

	Listening	Action	Change
	What pupils said needed changing or improving in relation to the ECM outcomes	**What pupils did to help to change and improve the Every Child Matters outcomes in school**	**What actually happened and changed as a result of pupil consultation and participation to improve ECM outcomes**
Adults	Key questions: ■ What did pupils want to happen and change in relation to ECM in school? ■ Whom did the pupils consult with, speak to? ■ Who in school listened to the pupils' views about how to improve ECM outcomes for pupils? ■ What evidence have you gathered to demonstrate that the pupils' views about ECM were listened to?	Key questions: ■ How was it decided what would happen, e.g. what action to be taken to address pupils' views on improving ECM outcomes? ■ What activities and actions did the pupils, staff and other stakeholders undertake? ■ Who exactly was involved in addressing the ECM issues pupils raised? ■ What processes and systems were put in place to work towards acting on the pupils' views to improve the ECM outcomes?	Key questions: ■ List what has changed or improved in relation to the ECM outcomes as a result of pupil voice. ■ Outline briefly why and what is better in school in relation to ECM as a result of the action/activities undertaken. ■ What do the pupils and other significant stakeholders actually say about the impact of pupil voice and participation on effecting change for ECM?
Children and young people	■	■	■
Wider community	■	■	■

Source: adapted from The National Youth Agency (2005) *What's Changed. Participation Outcome Tool*, p. 2

Note: This table is to be used by a range of adult stakeholders, as well as by pupils separately, with the various findings and views compared and cross-checked.

* For more information please visit www.nya.org.uk/whatschanged.

Table 7.2 Making a positive contribution: pupil voice, participation and involvement

Brief outline of pupil voice activities this year: Impact on pupils' Every Child Matters (ECM) outcomes:	
Evidence of what pupils say about how they (you) are encouraged to have a say in ECM decision making: ■ ■ ■ ■ ■ ■ ■	**Pupils' priorities for Every Child Matters pupil voice activities in the next year:** ■ ■ ■ ■ ■ ■ ■
Rate your school by ticking ONE box, to show how well-developed pupil voice, participation and involvement is.	
Emerging (Vision) ☐	**Developing** (In progress) ☐	**Established** (Everyday practice) ☐
Use this separately with staff and pupils, and cross-check for similarities and differences. Evidence can contribute to the school's SEF.	

Table 7.3 Evaluation framework on pupil voice and participation

Pupil voice and participation activities	Evidence	Impact on improving pupils' ECM outcomes
Pupil voice and participation is inclusive and reflects the full diversity of the school's pupil population		
Pupils meet with others in an emotionally intelligent environment, which promotes and fosters pupil voice and participation		
Pupils have access to information in a range of child-friendly formats, which enables them to make informed choices and decisions		
Pupils know their rights and responsibilities in relation to having a 'voice' and choice in matters that affect them		
Pupils are consulted as to how they prefer to participate and have a 'voice'		
Pupils are always given constructive feedback by adults, as to why or why not their views and ideas have been taken up and acted upon		
Pupils contribute to key policy development and improvement planning, which helps to improve their learning, well-being and life in general within school		
Pupils play an active part in contributing to producing information and publicity material about aspects of the educational setting for parents/carers and new pupils		
Pupils are trained and supported in how to develop communication and participation skills to strengthen their 'voice'		
Pupils help and support each other to become more self-confident in having a 'voice' and influencing decision making		
Pupils have regular opportunities to have a say about the quality and effectiveness of the processes that are utilised to seek their views and participation		
Pupils have the opportunity to take on responsibility within the educational setting		
All adults working within the educational setting promote and encourage pupils to have a 'voice', and are always prepared to listen to their views		

A member of the senior leadership team is proactive in coordinating pupil voice and participation activities across the school		
Pupils are allocated a budget and other appropriate resources to support pupil voice and participation activities		
Pupils are encouraged to take part in appropriate pupil voice activities in the local community, as well as in regional and national activities and events		
Pupils have the opportunity to contribute to and participate in training events for staff, governors and parents/carers		
Pupils are invited to contribute to recruiting and appointing new staff to the children's workforce in school		
New and existing staff receive ongoing training in how to support and enhance pupil 'voice' and participation		
The school's policy and charter on pupil voice and participation is kept under regular review and engages pupils in the process		
Pupils contribute evidence to the school's self-evaluation form (SEF) on an annual basis		

What are your three key priorities for pupil voice and participation for the next year, as a result of your evaluation?

■
■
■

Source: Adapted from Wirral MBC (2006) Charter of Participation for Children and Young People in Wirral, Section 3: 15–23

Table 7.4 Framework for evaluating the conditions of pupil voice and for assessing the meaningfulness of pupil involvement

Speaking	■ Who is allowed to speak? ■ To whom are they allowed to speak? ■ What are they allowed to speak about? ■ What language is allowed or encouraged?
Listening	■ Who is listening? ■ Why are they listening? ■ How are they listening?
Skills	■ Are the skills of dialogue encouraged and supported through training or other appropriate means? ■ Are these skills understood, developed and practical in the context of democratic values and dispositions? ■ Are those skills themselves transformed by those values and dispositions?
Attitudes and dispositions	■ How do those involved regard each other? ■ To what degree are the principles of equal value and the dispositions of care felt reciprocally and demonstrated through the reality of daily encounter?
Systems	■ How often does dialogue and encounter in which pupil voice is centrally important occur? ■ Who decides? ■ How do the systems enshrining the value and necessity of pupil voice mesh with or relate to other organisational arrangements (particularly those involving adults)?
Organisational culture	■ Do the cultural norms and values of the school proclaim the centrality of pupil voice within the context of education as a shared responsibility and shared achievement? ■ Do the practices, traditions and routine daily encounters demonstrate values supportive of pupil voice?
Spaces and the making of meaning	■ Where are the public spaces (physical and metaphorical) in which these encounters might take place? ■ Who controls them? ■ What values shape their being and their use?
Action	■ What action is taken? ■ Who feels responsible? ■ What happens if aspirations and good intentions are not realised?
The future	■ Do we need new structures? ■ Do we need new ways of relating to others?

Source: M. Fielding 2001, *Forum* 43(2): 100–109

Table 7.5 Evidence of the impact of pupil voice on effecting school change for Every Child Matters

Nature and focus of pupil voice activity, with date	Pupils involved, e.g. KS, year group, subgroups	Impact on ECM outcome Be Healthy	Impact on ECM outcome Stay Safe	Impact on ECM outcome Enjoy and Achieve	Impact on ECM outcome Make a Positive Contribution	Impact on ECM outcome Achieve Economic Well-being

Table 7.6 Impact of pupil voice in contributing to whole school change

Nature of pupil voice activity, date, pupil group involved	Impact of pupil voice on Changes in organisational practices, services and facilities	Impact of pupil voice on Strategy and Policy development	Impact on pupil voice on Budgetary decision making	Impact of pupil voice on Staff recruitment practices	Impact of pupil voice on the Production of materials and information resources

Table 7.7 Collecting the views of pupils

Pupil group: _____

Context:

Evidence		What the pupils' views tell you about:
In what ways are you gathering pupil voice and views?	How often in the school year are you seeking pupils' views?	Standards:
		Personal development:
Examples of actions taken based on pupils' views	Impact and effectiveness of actions taken	ECM well-being:
		Quality of provision:
How do you share the findings of pupil voice with pupils and other stakeholders?		

Source: Adapted from Leicestershire County Council 2005, *School Self Evaluation Toolkit. Section 2: Gathering the Views of Stakeholders*

Table 7.8 Knowing pupils' views

SEF Section 2: What are the views of pupils (learners) and how do you know?	School SEF OFSTED Grade (1–4) ☐
1. Present key outcomes of pupil voice	2. Sources of evidence of pupil voice	3. Summary of pupil voice strengths and weaknesses Strengths: Weaknesses:
4. Actions taken to improve pupil voice	5. Future priorities for pupil voice in relation to learning and ECM well-being	6. Future priorities for pupil voice in relation to provision

Source: Adapted from Leicestershire County Council 2005, *School Self Evaluation Toolkit. Section 2: SEF Summary Chart*

Glossary

Active listening – is a non-judgemental way of listening that focuses entirely on what the pupil is saying and confirming understanding of both the content of the message and the emotions and feelings underlying the message to ensure accurate understanding.

Change – is a process designed to improve practice, introduce new policies and functions, and is a significant alteration to existing practice.

Child – is defined as someone under the age of 14.

Circle time – is a group activity where pupils sit together in a circle formation with the purpose of furthering their understanding of themselves and others in the group.

Collaboration – is the process of working jointly with others, including those with whom one is not normally or immediately connected, to develop and achieve common goals.

Consultation – is the systematic process of seeking information by talking about things that matter with pupils, and listening to the opinions of children and young people on an issue or topic.

Emotional intelligence – refers to the ability to develop emotional sensitivity as well as the capacity to learn healthy emotional management skills.

Engagement – is the excitement, enthusiasm and investment an individual feels towards an aspect or issue that interests them.

Evaluation – is concerned with gauging and judging effectiveness, strengths and weaknesses, and interpreting how well things are going.

Hot seating – means putting an individual in a challenging, difficult or uncomfortable situation, and subjecting them to a series of unknown questions and investigation.

Human rights – are the basic rights and freedoms that belong to every person in the world, that are based on the core principles of dignity, fairness, equality, respect and autonomy.

Inclusion – concerns the quality of children and young people's experience; how they are helped to learn, achieve and participate fully in the life of the school.

Involvement – is the process of engaging pupils as partners in school improvement for the purpose of strengthening their commitment to education, community or democracy.

Outcomes – refers to identifiable (positive or negative) impact of interventions strategies or services on children and young people. It also refers to the five Every Child Matters well-being outcomes.

Participation – means committing to something worthwhile with opportunities to be engaged in decision making.

Personalisation – is where users (children, young people, families) are active participants in the shaping, development and delivery of education and related services.

Personalised learning – is the process of tailoring and matching teaching and learning around the way different pupils learn in order to meet their individual needs, interests and aptitudes to enable them to reach their optimum potential.

Pupil Referral Unit – is any centre maintained by an English local authority that provides alternative suitable and appropriate education for children and young people who are not able to attend a mainstream or special school.

Pupil voice – means pupils having the opportunity to have a say in decisions that affect them, and in what happens within school.

Self-evaluation – is a developmental, in-depth, reflective, collaborative process at the heart of school improvement, focused on the quality of children and young people's learning, achievement, personal development and well-being.

Vulnerable children – are all those children and young people who are at risk of social exclusion or who are disadvantaged and whose life chances are at risk if action is not taken to meet their needs. These children and young people include those who are looked-after children in public care; children with learning difficulties and disabilities; travellers, asylum seekers; excluded pupils; truants; young offenders; young family carers; children living in families where parents have mental illness, alcohol and drug dependency problems; children affected by domestic violence.

Well-being – means having the basic things you need to live and be healthy, safe and happy.

Welfare – refers to child safety issues and child protection.

Young person – this is someone who is aged between 14 and 17.

Useful Websites

www.childline.org.uk

www.childrenscommissioner.org

http://childrens-research-centre.open.ac.uk/

www.consultingpupils.co.uk

www.crae.org.uk

www.crights.org.uk

www.dcsf.gov.uk/timetotalk

www.11MILLION.org.uk

www.everychildmatters.gov.uk

www.4Children.org.uk/shoutout

www.goodchildhood.org.uk

www.investorsinpupils.co.uk/index.php

www.mylife.uk.com

www.ncsl.org.uk/ecm

www.nya.org.uk/actbyright

www.nya.org.uk/hearbyright

www.ofsted.gov.uk

www.participationforschools.org.uk

www.participationworks.org.uk

www.primaryreview.org.uk

www.pupil-voice.org.uk/resources.html

www.rights4me.org

www.savethechildren.org.uk/en/54_2355.htm

www.schoolcouncils.org

www.schoolcouncilswales.org.uk

www.soundout.org

www.studentvoice.co.uk

www.tda.gov.uk/remodelling

www.teachers.tv

Teachers' TV Pupil Voice Week 10–16 September 2007, series of pupil focus video programmes to watch online or download

www.uncrc.info

www.unhchr.ch/html/menu3/b/k2crc.htm

www.unicef.org/crc

www.unicef.org.uk/tz/teacher_support/rrs_award.asp

www.unicef.org.uk/youthvoice

www.unicef.org.uk/tz/resources/assets/pdf/join_up_ecm_uncrc.pdf

www.wiredforhealth.gov.uk/participationguidance

www.youthparliament.org.uk

www.young-voice.org

References and Further Reading

Alston, P., Tobin, J. and Darrow, M. (2005) *Laying the Foundations for Children's Rights. An Independent Study of Some Key Legal and Institutional Aspects of the Impact of the Convention on the Rights of the Child.* Florence: UNICEF.

Bloom, A. (2007) 'Headteacher for the Day? It'll Be a Cakewalk', *Times Educational Supplement,* London, 23 November 2007, p. 12.

Brighouse, T. (2006) *Essential Pieces. The Jigsaw of a Successful School.* Oxford: RM.

BT/ChildLine (2002) *Are Young People Being Heard?* London: British Telecommunications and ChildLine.

BT/UKYP (2004) *Seen and Heard 2.* London: British Telecommunications and the United Kingdom Youth Parliament.

Burke, C. (2003) *The School I'd Like: Children and Young People's Reflections on an Education for the 21st Century.* Abingdon: Routledge Falmer.

Cambridgeshire Children's Fund/Save the Children (2005) *Are You Listening! A Toolkit for Evaluating Children's Fund Services with Children and Young People.* Cambridge: Cambridgeshire Children's Fund and Save the Children.

Charlton, T. (1996) 'The Voice of the Child in School: Listening to Pupils in Classrooms and Schools', in Davie, R. and Galloway, D. *Listening to Children in Education.* London: David Fulton Publishers.

Cheminais, R. (2007) *Extended Schools and Children's Centres. A Practical Guide.* London: Routledge.

ChildLine (2002) *Rights of Children and Young People.* ChildLine Information Sheet 10. London: ChildLine.

Children's Society (2006) *Good Childhood: Question of our Times. A National Inquiry Launch Report.* London: The Children's Society.

Children's Society (2007a) *Good Childhood: What You Told Us about Friends.* London: The Children's Society.

Children's Society (2007b) *Good Childhood: What You Told Us about Family.* London: The Children's Society.

Children's Society (2007c) *Good Childhood: What You Told Us about Learning.* London: The Children's Society.

Clarke, A. (2005) 'Listening to the Pupil Voice', in *Teaching Expertise,* www.teachingexpertise.com/articles/listening-pupil-voice-211, accessed 01.03.2008.

CRAE (2007) *Ready, Steady, Change. Rights and the Law.* London: Children's Rights Alliance for England.

Cruddas, L. (2006) 'Engaged Voices – Dialogue Interaction and the Construction of Shared Social Meanings', in *Educational Action Research*, 15(3), pp. 479–88.

CSCi (2007) *Policy by Children. A Children's Views Report.* Newcastle-upon-Tyne: Commission for Social Care Inspection.

Cullingford, C. (1991) *The Inner World of the School.* London: Cassell.

CYPU (2001) *Learning to Listen. Core Principles for the Involvement of Children and Young People.* London: Children and Young People's Unit, Department for Education and Skills.

Davies, L. and Yamashita, H. (2007) *School Councils – School Improvement.* The London Secondary School Councils Action Research Project. Birmingham: Centre for International Education and Research (CIER), School of Education, University of Birmingham.

DCSF (2007a) *Report of the Findings from the DCSF 'Time to Talk' Consultation Activities.* London: Department for Children, Schools and Families.

DCSF (2007b) *Children and Young People Today: Evidence to Support the Development of the Children's Plan.* London: Department for Children, Schools and Families.

DCSF (2007c) *The Children's Plan. Building Brighter Futures – Summary.* Norwich: The Stationery Office.

DCSF (2007d) *Every Parent Matters.* London: Department for Children, Schools and Families.

DCSF (2007e) *Setting up a Parent Council: A Resource Pack.* London: Department for Children, Schools and Families.

DfES (2003) *Every Child Matters.* London: Department for Education and Skills.

DfES/NCB (2003) *Building a Culture of Participation. Involving Children and Young People in Policy, Service Planning, Delivery and Evaluation Handbook.* Nottingham: Department for Education and Skills, National Children's Bureau.

DfES (2004a) *Every Child Matters: Next Steps.* London: Department for Education and Skills.

DfES (2004b) *Working Together: Giving Children and Young People a Say.* London: Department for Education and Skills.

DfES (2004c) *Promoting Children and Young People's Participation through the National Healthy School Standard.* London: Department for Education and Skills.

DH/DfEE (2000) *National Healthy School Standard. Pupil Involvement.* Wetherby: Department of Health/Department for Education and Employment.

DH/DfES (2004) *National Healthy School Standard. Promoting Emotional Health and Wellbeing.* Wetherby: Department of Health/Department for Education and Skills.

East Sussex County Council (2007) *Pupil Voice: An Individual to Whole School Approach.* Cambridge: Widgit Software.

ESRC (2001) *Schools Ought to Be Happy Places.* Communicating – Consulting Pupils Project Newsletter No. 2. September 2001, p. 3. Cambridge: Economic and Social Research Council.

ESRC (2002a) *Using Image-Based Techniques in Researching Pupil Perspectives.* Communicating – Consulting Pupils Project Newsletter No. 5. May 2002, pp. 2–3. Cambridge: Economic and Social Research Council.

ESRC (2003a) *What Makes a Good Lesson and a Good Teacher?* Communicating – Consulting Pupils Project Newsletter No. 8, February 2003, pp. 2–3. Cambridge: Economic and Social Research Council.

ESRC (2003b) *Consulting through Questionnaires.* Communicating – Consulting Pupils Project Newsletter No. 9, pp. 1–3. Cambridge: Economic and Social Research Council.

ESRC (2004) *How We Feel about Learning – A Student Research Project.* Communicating – Consulting Pupils Project Newsletter No. 13, pp. 3–5. Cambridge: Economic and Social Research Council.

ESSA (2007) *Citizens' Juries in Schools and Colleges.* London: English Secondary Students' Association.

Fielding, M. (2001) 'Beyond the Rhetoric of Student Voice: New Departures or New Constraints in the Transformation of 21st Century Schooling?', *Forum*, 43(2), pp. 100–09. Cambridge.

Fielding, M. (2004) ' "New Wave" Student Voice and the Renewal of Civic Society', *London Review of Education, Special issue on 'Education for Civic Society'*, 2(3), pp. 197–217.

Fletcher, A. (2004) *Meaningful Student Involvement: Guide to Students as Partners in School Change.* Olympia Washington: Soundout.

Flutter, J. and Rudduck, J. (2004) *Consulting Pupils: What's in It for Schools?* London: Routledge Falmer.

4Children (2007) *My Shout Out. The Buzz Survey.* London: 4Children.

Frankel, H. (2007) 'This Is What We Suggest', *TES Magazine*, 19 October. London: Times Educational Supplement.

Frost, B. and Rogers, J. (2006) *Every Child Matters: Empowering the Student Voice.* London: National Teacher Research Panel/DfES Innovation Unit.

Gunter, H. and Thompson, P. (2007) 'Learning about Student Voice, Support for Learning', *British Journal of Learning Support*, 22(4), p. 181.

Hadfield, M. and Haw, K. (2004) 'Aspects of Voice', *NEXUS*, 7, pp. 24–5. Nottingham: National College of School Leadership.

Halsey, K. Murfield, J., Harland, J.L. and Lord, P. (2007) *The Voice of Young People: An Engine for Improvement? Scoping the Evidence.* Slough: Centre for British Teachers/National Foundation for Educational Research.

Hampshire County Council (2001) *Children's Learning: A Model for Self-Evaluation.* Winchester: Hampshire Inspection and Advisory Service.

Hargreaves, D. (2004) *Personalising Learning 2. Student Voice and Assessment for Learning.* London: SHA/Specialist Schools Trust.

Hart, R. (1992) *Children's Participation from Tokenism to Citizenship.* Innocenti Essays No. 4. Florence: UNICEF International Child Development Centre.

Hastings, S. (2003) *The Issue: Pupil Power.* London: Times Educational Supplement.

Hayes, B. (2002) 'Community Cohesion and Inclusive Education', *Educational and Child Psychology*, 19(4), pp. 75–90.

Hobbs, C. (2005) 'Professional consultation with pupils through teaching and learning'. (D.Ed. Psy. dissertation, Newcastle-upon-Tyne)

Howard League for Penal Reform (2007a) *Children as Victims: Child-Sized Crimes in a Child-Sized World.* London: The Howard League for Penal Reform.

Howard League for Penal Reform (2007b) *News Release,* 10 October, www.howarleague.org accessed on 10/10/2007.

Jackson, D. (2004) 'Why Pupil Voice?', *NEXUS,* 7, Nottingham: National College of School Leadership.

Johnson, K. (2004) *Children's Voices: Pupil Leadership in Primary Schools.* Nottingham: National College of School Leadership.

Kirby, P., Lanyon, C., Cronin, K. and Sinclair, R. (2003) *Building a Culture of Participation. Involving Children and Young People in Policy, Service Planning, Delivery and Evaluation Handbook.* London: Department for Education and Skills.

Klein, R. (2003) *We Want our Say: Children as Active Participants in their Education.* Stoke on Trent: Trentham Books.

Leicestershire County Council (2005) *School Self Evaluation Toolkit. Section 2: Gathering the Views of Stakeholders.* Leicester: School Improvement and Performance Service.

Leicestershire County Council (2005) *School Self Evaluation Toolkit. Section 2: SEF Summary Chart.* Leicester: School Improvement and Performance Service.

Levin, B. (1999) 'Putting Students at the Centre in Education Reform', *International Journal of Educational Change,* 1(2), pp. 155–72(18).

LSC (2002) *Investors in Pupils – The Indicators.* Coventry: Learning and Skills Council.

Macbeath, J., Demetriou, H., Ruddock, J. and Myers, K. (2003) *Consulting Pupils: A Toolkit for Teachers.* Cambridge: Pearson Publishing.

Margo, J., Dixon, M., Pearce, N. and Reed, H. (2006) *Freedom's Orphans. Raising Youth in a Changing World.* Institute of Public Policy.

Matthews, H. (2001) *Children and Community Regeneration.* London: Groundwork/Save the Children.

Mayall, B. (2007) *Children's Lives outside School and their Educational Impact.* Primary Review Research Survey 8/1. Cambridge: University of Cambridge Faculty of Education.

McIntyre, D., Pedder, D., and Ruddock, J. (2005) *Pupil Voice: Comfortable and Uncomfortable Learning for Teachers.* Research Paper in Education 20(2), pp. 149–68. Cambridge: University of Cambridge.

NASEN (2004) *Policy on Pupil Participation.* Tamworth: National Association for Special Educational Needs.

NCB (2007) *How to Involve Children and Young People in Recruitment and Selection. Participation Works.* London: National Children's Bureau.

NYA (2005) *Hear by Right. Standards for the Active Involvement of Children and Young People. Mapping and planning tool.* London: National Youth Agency.

OFSTED (2007a) *Making Contact Point Work. Children's Views on the Government Guidance. A Report by the Children's Rights Director for England.* London: Office for Standards in Education, Children's Services and Skills.

OFSTED (2007b) *National Summary TellUs2 Survey.* London: Office for Standards in Education, Children's Services and Skills.

OFSTED (2007c) *Self-Evaluation Form for Primary Schools (with and without Nursery Provision), Middle Schools (Deemed Primary)*. London: Office for Standards in Education, Children's Services and Skills.

Palmer, S. (2006) *Toxic Childhood. How the Modern World is Damaging our Children and What We Can Do about It*. London: Orion.

QCA (2006) *A Student Democracy*. London: Qualifications and Curriculum Authority.

Robinson, C. and Fielding, M. (2007) *Children and their Primary Schools: Pupils' Voices*. Primary Review Research Survey 5/3. Cambridge: University of Cambridge Faculty of Education.

Ruddock, J. (2003) *Pupil Voice and Citizenship Education. A Report for the QCA Citizenship and PSHE Team*. Cambridge: Faculty of Education, University of Cambridge.

Ruddock, J. (2004) *Pupil Voice is Here to Stay!* London: Qualifications and Curriculum Authority.

Save the Children (2005a) *The Recruitment Pack. Involving Children and Young People in the Selection of Staff*. Edinburgh: Save the Children.

Save the Children (2005b) *Something to Say. Listening to Children: Developing an Anti-Bullying Culture in Primary Schools*. Belfast: Save the Children.

Save the Children (2006) *Children's Rights: A Teacher's Guide*. London: Save the Children.

School Councils UK (2005a) *Activity Guide 04. Evaluating Your School Council*. London: School Councils UK.

School Councils UK (2005b) *Activity Guide 05. Student Governors (England)*. London: School Councils UK.

School Councils UK (2006) *School Councils UK Briefing. School Councils and Every Child Matters*. London: School Councils UK.

School Councils UK (2007) *School Councils UK Briefing. School Councils UK Response to Real Decision Making? School Councils in Action*. London: School Councils UK.

Shier, H. (2001) 'Pathways to Participation: Openings, Opportunities and Obligations – A New Model for Enhancing Children's Participation in Decision-Making', *Children and Society*, 15, pp. 107–17.

Spender, B. (2006) 'Introducing Every Child Matters – Routes through the Curriculum', *Curriculum Management Update*, November. London: Optimus Publishing.

Stewart, W. (2007) 'More Children to Judge Teachers', *Times Educational Supplement*, 21 September 2007.

TDA (2007a) *Consultation Toolkit. Community Consultation Tools to Support the Development of Extended Services*. London: Training and Development Agency for Schools.

TDA (2007b) *School Improvement Planning Framework. Putting the Child at the Centre of School Improvement Planning. Overview*. London: Training and Development Agency for Schools.

Teaching and Learning in 2020 Review Group (2006) *2020 Vision: Report of the Teaching and Learning in 2020 Review Group*. London: DfES.

The Joseph Rowntree Foundation (2007) *Parenting and the Different Ways it Affects Children's Lives – Children's Voice in Ordinary Families*. York: The Joseph Rowntree Foundation.

The National Youth Agency (2005a) *Involving Children and Young People – An Introduction*. Leicester: National Youth Agency.

The National Youth Agency (2005b) *What's Changed? Participation Outcomes Tool. For Use by Children and Young People.* Leicester: National Youth Agency.

The Primary Review (2007) *Community Soundings: The Primary Review Regional Witness Sessions.* Cambridge: University of Cambridge.

Todd, L. (2007) *Partnerships for Inclusive Education. A Critical Approach to Collaborative Working.* London: Routledge.

Twist, C., Schagen, I., and Hodgson, C. (2007) *Readers and Reading: The National Report for England 2006.* (PIRLS: Progress in International Reading Literacy Study) Slough: NFER.

UNICEF (2006) *Every Child Matters. The Five Outcomes and the UN Convention on the Rights of the Child (UNCRC).* London: UNICEF UK.

UNICEF (2007a) *Report Card 7, Child Poverty in Perspective: An Overview of Child Well-being in Rich Countries.* Rome: UNICEF Innocenti Research Centre.

UNICEF (2007b) *Rights Respecting School Award Introduction.* London: UNICEF UK.

United Nations Convention on the Rights of the Child (UNCRC) (1989) Geneva: United Nations.

Whitty, G. and Wisby, E. (2007) *Real Decision Making? School Councils in Action.* DCSF Research Report 001. London: Institute of Education, University of London.

Wirral Metropolitan Borough Council (2006) *Charter of Participation for Children and Young People in Wirral.* Birkenhead: Wirral Children's Fund and On Track.

Index

Page numbers in *italics* refer to tables and figures.